Accompaniments

Accompaniments

Chutneys, Relishes, Pickles, Sambals, and Preserves

Kusuma Cooray

A Latitude 20 Book

UNIVERSITY OF HAWAI'I PRESS

HONOLULU

24 23 22 21 20 19   6 5 4 3 2 1

Library of Congress Cataloging-in-Publication Data

Names: Cooray, Kusuma, author.
Title: Accompaniments : chutneys, relishes, pickles, sambals, and preserves /
   Kusuma Cooray.
Description: Honolulu : University of Hawai'i Press, [2019] | "A latitude 20
   book." | Includes bibliographical references and index.
Identifiers: LCCN 2019019195 | ISBN 9780824867942 (pbk. ; alk. paper)
Subjects: LCSH: Side dishes (Cooking) | LCGFT: Cookbooks.
Classification: LCC TX819.A1 C658 2019 | DDC 641.81—dc23
LC record available at https://lccn.loc.gov/2019019195

Food styling by Kusuma Cooray
Food photography by Rico Gatdula
Cover photos by Rico Gatdula
Design by Mardee Melton

LOVINGLY DEDICATED TO

Ranjit George Cooray

Contents

Foreword by John Morton   ix

Acknowledgments   xi

Introduction   xiii

How to Use This Book   xvii

CHUTNEYS   1

RELISHES   27

PICKLES   97

SAMBALS   147

PRESERVES   195

How to Use Spices   223

An Essential Glossary   229

Index   253

Foreword

I have had the privilege of working with Chef Kusuma Cooray for more than twenty-five years. I have admired her as she shared her love of the cuisine of her native Sri Lanka with students and showed them how to blend the traditional tastes of South Asia into modern, multicultural culinary treats. Her first two cookbooks extend this knowledge to the home cook, and I eagerly have sought to learn how to at least approximate the goodness I had experienced at her table. Yet there seemed to be a missing piece. Now, in this third cookbook, Chef Cooray completes the puzzle and highlights the importance of accompaniments in creating a complete dish.

An accompaniment may sound like something that simply tags along, a little something extra to put on the plate. The notion is far from the truth. The reality is that the various chutneys, relishes, pickles, sambals, and preserves enhance and complement the other items on the plate. Sometimes they enhance and strengthen a flavor. Other times they enhance or provide a contrast in taste or texture. In all cases they work in concert with the featured dish to create a more complex, more enjoyable dining experience. Change the accompaniment and you change the experience.

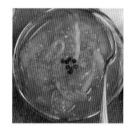

I remember the conversations my wife and I would have after one of Chef Cooray's fabulous meals, and they were often as much about the delicious accompaniment as the rest of the plate. This third cookbook will help readers understand not just how to prepare these various accompaniments but more importantly how to use them, how to integrate them with the meal, how to adapt the spices and the tastes, and, in Chef Cooray's words, how to take the main dish from ordinary to heavenly. Enjoy!

John Morton
Vice President for Community Colleges, University of Hawai'i

Acknowledgments

Many helped me put this book together. This is my third book with the University of Hawai'i Press, and I thank my editor, Masako Ikeda, once again for her guidance, encouragement, and assistance. My sincere gratitude to Carol Abe, marketing manager, for her constant help in promoting my books. Thank you to Steve Hirashima, for the friendship and aloha he has always extended to me. Thank you to Danny Li, in sales, who offered his help whenever I asked. Thank you to all at the University of Hawai'i Press for the gracious support extended to me since I started working with them in 1998.

I am grateful to Dr. John Morton, Vice President for Community Colleges, who has been there for me for all the significant milestones in my professional career. A sincere thank you for their enthusiastic support to the following people at Kapi'olani Community College: Ron Takahashi, chair, Culinary Arts Department, to whom I go when I need help; Dr. Leon Richards, former chancellor; and Dr. Carl Hefner, chair, Social Sciences. Thank you and aloha to Susan Pope, for performing the tedious task of indexing.

My photographer, the talented Rico Gatdula of HawaiiPro-Photo, painstakingly gave life to my work through nearly a hundred photographs for this book. His photographs also adorn *Ocean to Plate,* my second, award-winning book. Rico has been in my life for a long time, generously provided me with assistance, photographed major highlights in my career, and aided me when I needed his expert help. Lisa van der Spoel, one of my outstanding students, did the metric calculations for this book as she did for *Ocean to Plate;* thank you, Lisa, for your dedication and hard work.

I am honored to have Laura Iwasaki copyedit my book. My sincere thanks to you, Laura. Many thanks to Kristy Kiesel, the computer expert I relied on during the process of producing the manuscript, and to Sanath De Silva and Thilakshi Amarasinghe, who assisted me with reviewing the manuscript online in Sri Lanka. My sincere thanks to Sally Yamaguchi, Culinary Arts Department office manager, who was always there for me when I needed assistance.

A special thank you to Chef Dan Wetter, Chef David Brown, Chef Warren Uchida, Chef Grant Sato, and Chef Dave Hamada for their friendship and aloha. Finally, I appreciate the good wishes from friends and family who are far away in many parts of the world.

To my special friends here at home in Hawai'i, who have been constantly present in my life, thank you for your support, encouragement, and love. I could not have made it without you!

Introduction

How true. I was born and raised in Sri Lanka, fondly known as the "Pearl of the Indian Ocean," and grew up in a comfortable home with loving parents and four siblings. Food was a big part of our lives. I was only nine years old when I started my "apprenticeship" in my own home under the watchful eyes of kitchen helpers. I learned how to cook, not so much with the spectrum of taste and its intriguing flavor sensations, but with the fragrances of herbs and spices.

Sri Lankan and Indian cuisines are the most aromatic of all cuisines. Their captivating flavors and fragrances are unparalleled, and these tastes are a big part of me, who I am, and what I do. I traveled, studied, and apprenticed in England and in France, where I experienced the taste and grandeur of French food. In doing so, I discovered new ingredients and techniques, new flavors and textures. The French preparations and garnishes were fascinating; taste sensations were unreal. And they still live with me. Building on knowledge I had gained as a "child apprentice," I continued to learn and appreciate flavors from around the world. My study of the characteristics of individual herbs and spices enabled me to appreciate them better.

My late husband, Ranjit, and I decided to make the great island state of Hawai'i our home, and it is now a big part of my life. In multiethnic Hawai'i, Asian Pacific cuisine evolved with seafood as a central focus. My first taste of ocean-fresh raw fish happened here. I soon came to enjoy Hawaiian food and became good at preparing it, too. In the past, I was the executive chef of the famous restaurant The Willows, where we served what I proudly think of as the best of Hawaiian food. I was fortunate to have taught at the University of Hawai'i's Culinary Institute of the Pacific. Hawai'i is truly blessed, with its bounty of seafood, exotic fruits, and farm-fresh vegetables. They inspired me to formulate the recipes for this book, which celebrate the ingenious use of herbs and spices with the bounty of Hawai'i. The recipes reflect my appreciation of what Hawai'i has generously offered me—friendly people and their aloha, the fresh air and water, the warm Hawaiian sun, and especially the beautiful sunsets!

The structure of our taste starts very early in life.

MARK MILLER, chef
Red Sage, Washington, DC

This book contains recipes I love and enjoy cooking. Some of the recipes and spicing styles are unique and true to my heritage. Some preparations are elaborate. But they are all delicious and easy to make. Most importantly, my purpose is to bring the special flavors of the bounty of the Hawaiian Islands to the table.

Traditionally, food items added to a dish in order to enhance flavor were known as condiments, as in the case of simple American mustard, ketchup, and pickles. Today accompaniments are a favorite category of food that is commonly used around the world to add flavor to a dish; they are very different from the condiments of the past. Accompaniments can be cooked or uncooked preparations and sometimes are referred to as relishes. They make eating more pleasurable.

Chutneys, relishes, pickles, sambals, and preserves are culinary delights and are generally known as accompaniments. Most of the appealing accompaniments come from Asia—especially from India, Pakistan, Sri Lanka, and Indonesia. It is well known that food has been influenced through the ages by the South Asian use of spices. Accompaniments that originate from these countries have assertive and bold flavors, intriguing fragrances and aromas, and an enticing appearance. Some are cooling and soothe palates; some are hot and awaken appetites. These are palate teasers that take a main dish from ordinary to heavenly. Thus they are as important as the main dish. They are served not only as accompaniments to certain foods but also as essential components of main dishes or meals. For example, an Indian or Sri Lankan meal of rice and curry is incomplete without a dollop of chutney, relish, pickles, or sambal. The number and variety of these taste-tingling morsels set these meals apart. The addition of simple accompaniments such as **Mint and Coconut Relish** (p. 63) and crisp fried poppadum will make every mouthful of even a simple meal flavorful and satisfying.

Accompaniments are not limited to rice and curry and breads but may be used with Western main dishes, too. I create menus with accompaniments that add accents of color, texture, and fragrance to dishes. While these accents are flavor enhancing, spices are what make these delicacies unique. Besides their fragrance, spices impart mystique to food; they also have medicinal and curative values. Asafetida, a spice, was a popular condiment in Rome during the first century. It was a favorite of Roman gourmet Marcus Gavius Apicius. It still is a favorite in India but is not commonly used in Sri Lanka. Although it is known for its anti-flatulence properties,

I use it for its mystical aroma rather than for its health benefits. Asafetida is available in health food stores and specialty grocery stores in cities around the world. As a general rule, spices stimulate appetite and are thought to enhance blood circulation. Cloves and turmeric are known for their antiseptic properties. The combination of coriander and ginger is believed to act as a decongestant.

Accompaniments are always served in small portions. Some relishes, such as **Fruit "Chaat Masala"** (p. 29), are presented as appetizers or salads and side dishes. **Rhubarb and Green Apple Preserve** (p. 213) is served as an accompaniment to roast pork or lamb and as a topping for coconut ice cream. Some preserves, such as **Spicy Winter Melon Preserve** (p. 204), accompany poultry dishes, while others, such as **Brandied Cherries** (p. 220), are good to enjoy on their own.

Generally, chutneys can last a long time. For example, once opened, jars of **Hawaiian Mango Chutney** (p. 2) and **Green Mango Chutney** (p. 3) can be refrigerated for three to four weeks. In contrast, relishes and sambals must be used quickly. They have poor keeping qualities, so they are made in smaller quantities. **Hot Green Cilantro Relish** (p. 37), for example, has to be used soon after preparation. Some of these items can be refrigerated for a day or two only. Generally, pickles, especially sun-dried pickles, can last as long as ten to twelve years. In fact, pickles improve with age. **Hot and Spicy Lime Pickles** (p. 101) could last for six to eight months.

Some of these preparations are available commercially. However, it is exciting to use seasonal foods in innovative ways and make them yourself. Sustainability is survival for many, and we can help our farmers by using local produce. Almost all fruits, vegetables, and some flowers—especially Hawai'i's underutilized fruits and vegetables—can be made into delicious preserves.

How to Use This Book

The aim of this book is to share recipes for accompaniments and guide the reader through the process of making them. It is written in a simple style and provides explicit instructions that are easy to understand and follow. I advise the reader to go over the introduction and the recipes before beginning to cook from this book. Herbs and spices are listed along with their characteristics in the glossary. It is important to know the characteristics and properties of spices and how to use them, since they are used to flavor most of the recipes. All ingredients listed in recipes are available in most large city markets and ethnic markets; Indian and health food stores stock many of the spices as well.

I provide all measures in both US and metric units and measure amounts by both weight and volume. Volume is commonly used for liquids and for dry and wet ingredients such as sugar and chopped onions. Amounts of dry ingredients too small to weigh accurately are given in cups, tablespoons, and teaspoons. Although these are not as accurate as weight, the slight differences should not affect the finished dish. Please note that amounts, temperatures, and timing are provided as a guide, so please use your best judgment.

Recipes throughout the book call for vegetable oil, but where applicable, you may substitute the fat of your choice. My preference is olive oil. Black pepper used for seasoning should be understood as ground black pepper, freshly ground whenever possible. Amounts are not given for salt because salt should be used to your taste or the taste of those you're cooking for. I use whole milk yogurt, not nonfat or reduced fat yogurt. Onions used in recipes are brown onions, unless a recipe specifies green or red onions. Onions, shallots, garlic, and ginger should always be peeled, unless the recipe instructs otherwise. Substitutions are given in recipes or in the introductions to recipes.

Sizes of cookware and dishes are indicated in recipes as small, medium, and large. When a large pot or pan is essential, the recipe specifies and explains why. Heavy-bottomed pans are often recommended for preparing chutneys and preserves. Many recipes call for nonreactive utensils, dishes, and cookware (see the "Utensils and Equipment" section that follows). Special terms and unfamiliar herbs, spices, and ingredients are explained in the glossary.

Recipes include serving suggestions; however, there are countless ways for you to incorporate these delicacies into your menus as suits your taste.

Basics of Food Preparation

Wash fruits and vegetables under running water to get rid of all traces of dust and dirt. For preserves, it is particularly crucial to avoid any condition that will encourage the growth of bacteria. This starts with fresh, sound ingredients. As a general rule, fruits should be ripe or slightly underripe, not overripe, unless specified as such in a special recipe. Vegetables should be the same, mature enough but not old and tough. Fruits and vegetables must be dry before use; moisture encourages the growth of mold in preserves.

Utensils and Equipment

Nonreactive equipment and utensils should be used in food production and preservation. Use stainless steel knives and small tools for preparing fruits and vegetables. Stainless steel knives will not corrode but are harder to sharpen. Ceramic knives are excellent, but they are rather expensive. High-carbon stainless steel knives are the best and are less expensive than ceramic knives. They will not rust, corrode, or discolor and take an extremely sharp edge. Steel knives are traditional favorites in the kitchen because they can be honed to a very sharp edge, but they corrode and discolor easily when used with acidic fruits, onions, and some vegetables. They may also leave a metallic taste in food.

Common cookware includes pots, pans, woks, hotel pans, and molds. They can be made of metal (stainless steel, aluminum, copper, cast iron, etc.), glass, ceramic, and enamel. Nonstick cookware is marketed under many trade names, the most common being Teflon and Silverstone.

Pots are large round vessels with straight sides and two loop handles. They are available in a range of sizes and are used on the stovetop for stocks and soups or for boiling or simmering foods. Types of pots include the stockpot, the saucepot, and the straight-sided *sautoir*.

Pans are round vessels with one long handle and straight or sloped sides. These are usually smaller and shallower than pots. They are also available in a range of sizes and are used for general stovetop cooking, especially sautéing and frying (referred to as frying pans and sauté pans) or reducing liquids rapidly. These include the saucepan, cast iron skillet, *sauteuse* (shallow, with outward-sloping sides), and the *sautoir* and *rondeau* (also called a *brazier*), both slope-sided and shallower than pots.

Woks, originally used for Asian cooking, are now used in many professional kitchens and homes. Their rounded bottoms and curved sides diffuse heat and make it possible to stir or toss contents. The large domed lids help retain heat.

Hotel pans are rectangular stainless steel pans designed to hold food on steam tables for service. Molds are used in the oven.

Stainless steel does not react with food, unlike aluminum, but it is a poor heat conductor and tends to scorch food easily. More expensive stainless steel pots and pans are available with a heavy layer of copper or aluminum bonded to the underside. This feature combines the nonreactive advantage of stainless steel with the heat-conducting qualities of copper or aluminum.

Aluminum is the metal used most commonly in commercial utensils. Do not use aluminum containers for storing or aluminum cookware for preparing acidic foods because the metal reacts chemically with many foods.

Cast iron cookware distributes heat evenly and holds a high temperature well. It is often used for griddles and large skillets. Relatively inexpensive, cast iron is extremely heavy. It must be properly conditioned and kept dry to prevent rust. (A frying pan may be used instead of a cast iron skillet for roasting spices.)

Glass retains heat well but conducts it poorly. Glass cookware is rarely used in homes or commercial operations because of the danger of breakage.

Ceramics, including earthenware, and stoneware are used primarily in baking dishes. They are easily chipped and cracked and should not be set on direct heat; quick temperature changes cause the cookware to crack.

Enamel-lined pots and pans scratch and chip easily, creating hiding places for bacteria, and chipped gray enamel can cause food poisoning. Their use in commercial kitchens is prohibited by law.

Uncoated iron and copper cookware forms toxic substances when used with high-acid foods; uncoated aluminum darkens and causes deterioration in certain acidic foods. Nonstick cookware provides a slippery nonreactive finish that prevents food from sticking and allows the use of less fat in cooking. However, this kind of cookware needs a lot of care, as the coating can scratch or blister. Do not use metal utensils with nonstick cookware.

HAWAIIAN MANGO CHUTNEY

GREEN MANGO CHUTNEY

HAWAIIAN STAR FRUIT CHUTNEY

CITRUS CHUTNEY

BLACK PLUM CHUTNEY

PEACH CHUTNEY

FESTIVE FRUIT CHUTNEY

DATE CHUTNEY

TAMARIND AND RAISIN CHUTNEY

CRANBERRY AND ORANGE CHUTNEY

DRIED CRANBERRY CHUTNEY

WI APPLE CHUTNEY

HOT LIME PICKLES CHUTNEY

GOOSEBERRY CHUTNEY

PEAR AND GINGER CHUTNEY

PAPAYA CHUTNEY

TOMATO AND LEMON CHUTNEY

GREEN TOMATO CHUTNEY

GREEN TOMATO AND APRICOT CHUTNEY

KABOCHA CHUTNEY

CHUTNEYS

Of all accompaniments, chutney remains a favorite around the world. Chutneys are a relish, preserved by cooking. They are exotic and rich with distinctive spices. Most of the world's appealing chutneys come from South Asia: India, Pakistan, and Sri Lanka. In taste, they range from sweet to hot and spicy, sour and tangy to salty, creamy and soothing to fiery hot. The main ingredients vary and may include fresh fruits such as mangoes, pineapples, pears, peaches, guavas, and apples; dried fruits such as dates, apricots, and raisins; and vegetables such as tomatoes, pumpkins, onions, and carrots. Spices, ginger, garlic, red and green chilies, and herbs add flavor. Tamarind, vinegar, yogurt, citrus juice, sugar or jaggery, and salt are used appropriately. Marrying the flavors of fresh fruits and vegetables with those of nuts, seasonings, and spices produces a variety of unusual chutneys. Vinegar and sugar work well with spices and give cooked chutneys a lusciously thick, shiny texture and appearance. While these ingredients are all flavor enhancing, it is spices that make South Asian chutneys unique.

When preparing and cooking chutneys, use nonreactive utensils and equipment. Chutneys should be cooled, covered, and sealed in sterilized jars. Stored in this manner, a well-prepared chutney keeps for six months or so. Once a jar is opened, it should be refrigerated.

Hawaiian Mango Chutney

8 cups (2 L) (packed) mangoes, peeled and cut into pieces 1 inch (2.5 cm) long and 1 inch wide

Salt

3 cups (750 ml) apple cider vinegar

6 cups (1.5 L) light brown sugar

½ cup (125 ml) minced ginger

¼ cup (60 ml) minced garlic

¾ cup (180 ml) minced onion

5 to 6 finely chopped fresh Hawaiian chilies or cayenne pepper, to taste

3 teaspoons (15 ml) ground cinnamon

1 teaspoon (5 ml) ground nutmeg

1 teaspoon (5 ml) ground cloves

Hawaiian mangoes, also known as "common" mangoes, make a good chutney, as do many varieties of mangoes available in other parts of the world. Look for half-ripe mangoes just about to turn a light yellow color. These mangoes keep their shape and do not get mushy when sliced and cooked. Hawaiian chilies (also known as bird's eye chilies) are desirable for adding some heat to this chutney; use more or less according to your taste. Mango chutney is universally known as an accompaniment to rice and curry, but today it plays a much bigger role. Use it to top swirls of cream to garnish soups, add zest to sandwich fillings, adorn hors d'oeuvres, and fill fancy pastries. The uses for mango chutney and chutney in general are endless.

Directions

Place mango pieces in a large bowl. Sprinkle 1½ tablespoons of salt on the mangoes and set aside for at least 6 to 8 hours. Rinse mangoes in cold water, then place in a colander and drain well. Wipe remaining moisture off mango pieces with paper towels

Combine vinegar and sugar in a large *rondeau* and cook over high heat. When mixture begins to simmer, stir in ginger, garlic, onion, chilies, spices, and mangoes. Add a little more sugar if the mixture needs sweetness.

Continue to cook over low heat, stirring occasionally, and season with sugar and salt to taste. Simmer for about 1½ to 2 hours, or until mixture is thick and mangoes are translucent. Cool and store.

Yield: 1½ quarts (1½ L)

Green Mango Chutney

This mango chutney is not as spicy as Hawaiian Mango Chutney. It is sweet and sour, dense and sticky.

Directions

Place sliced mangoes in a large dish (with enough space to salt mangoes), sprinkle with 1 tablespoon salt, and mix together. Let sit in a warm kitchen for 24 hours. Rinse mango slices in cold water, then place in a colander and drain well. Wipe mango slices with paper towels.

In a blender, blend ginger, garlic, and chilies with ¼ cup (60 ml) of the vinegar until the mixture has a smooth consistency. Pour into a medium *sautoir*, add the remaining vinegar and the sugar, and place over medium heat. Bring to a simmer, add mangoes and cook for about 45 minutes. Add raisins halfway through and continue cooking, stirring occasionally, until mango slices are soft and translucent. Cool and store.

Yield: 1 pint (500 ml)

4 cups (1 L) peeled and sliced unripe green mangoes

Salt

1 tablespoon (15 ml) chopped ginger

1 tablespoon (15 ml) chopped garlic

2 teaspoons (30 ml) chopped chilies

1 cup (250 ml) apple cider vinegar

2 cups (500 ml) sugar

¼ cup (60 ml) light golden raisins

Hawaiian Star Fruit Chutney

Star fruit in general are sweet, but some varieties range from mildly tart to bland. They are full of water. The waxy-skinned, orange-to-lemony-yellow fruit is about 5 inches (12.7 cm) long and oval in shape, with five ribs that run down its length; a crosswise slice is shaped like a star. Use ripe fruit, sliced or diced, in fruit salads. Mature yet unripe fruit is best made into chutney. Star fruit does not need to be peeled; the skin is edible. Star fruit chutney is exceptional with grilled or sautéed fish, and slices of raw or briefly sautéed star fruit make an attractive garnish for cooked fish dishes.

12 large star fruit (about 1½ pounds [680 g])

2 tablespoons (30 ml) plus 1½ cups (375 ml) sugar

½ cup (125 ml) finely chopped onion

4 fresh red chilies, seeded and chopped

1 tablespoon (15 ml) finely chopped ginger

1 cup (250 ml) distilled vinegar

2-inch (5 cm) piece of cinnamon stick

Salt

Directions

Cut a thin slice off each end of the star fruit and trim the brownish edges off the five ribs. Cut trimmed fruit into spears, slice off seeds if any, and cut spears into small dice. Place star fruit in a nonreactive medium container, sprinkle with 2 tablespoons (30 ml) sugar, and toss. Set aside for 20 minutes. Strain released liquid and wipe fruit dry with paper towels.

Place 1½ cups sugar (adjusting to taste as necessary), onions, chilies, ginger, vinegar, and cinnamon stick in a medium saucepan and simmer over low heat for about 10 minutes. Fold in star fruit and season with salt to taste. Cook over medium heat for about 10 minutes. Remove and discard cinnamon stick. Cool and store.

Yield: 1 pint (500 ml)

Citrus Chutney

4 lemons, halved lengthwise and thinly sliced, seeds reserved

4 sour oranges (also known as bitter oranges and Seville oranges), quartered and thinly sliced, seeds reserved

2 sweet oranges, quartered and thinly sliced, seeds reserved

8 cups (2 L) water

Sugar, same weight as the weight of cooked fruit

½ cup (125 ml) lemon juice

1 cup (250 ml) apple cider vinegar

2 teaspoons (10 ml) cayenne pepper

1 tablespoon (15 ml) ground cloves

2 teaspoons (10 ml) ground mace

1 teaspoon (5 ml) ground cinnamon

2 teaspoons (10 ml) dried ginger powder

1 teaspoon (5 ml) coarsely ground cardamom seeds

2 teaspoons (10 ml) salt, or to taste

This is an elegant chutney that I use on special occasions for my family. It looks like a marmalade and is made the same way. Use this chutney with roasts or fancy rice and curries and as a garnish for lamb dishes, whether a rack of lamb or braised lamb shank. It is also a fabulous accompaniment to duck *à l'orange,* and don't forget to serve a little watercress dressed with a tart vinaigrette, as is traditional with the French. The chutney not only is delicious but also aids digestion.

Citrus fruits, especially their seeds, are high in pectin, which helps make chutney jell and glisten. Use different citrus fruits as desired, and the results will be similar. For example, tangerines, mandarins, and blood oranges all work well in this recipe.

As a rule of thumb, the weight of the sugar should be the same as the weight of the cooked fruit. Keep in mind, however, that it is always best to hold back some sugar, taste the chutney when the sugar has melted, and add more if needed.

Directions

Place sliced fruit in a medium bowl and the seeds in a smaller bowl. Pour water over both fruit and seeds and let soak for 24 hours.

Transfer fruit and its soaking water to a large *rondeau.* The lemon slices should have enough room to sit in the liquid without break-ing. Strain seeds, saving soaking water and adding to the *rondeau.* Tie seeds in a sachet and add to the pan. Bring contents to a boil, then lower heat and simmer gently for 2 hours.

Remove and discard sachet. Remove cooked fruit from the *rondeau,* weigh, and set aside, reserving pan. Weigh out sugar, add to the pan, and simmer over low heat, stirring continuously until sugar is dissolved. Add cooked fruit and remaining ingredients. Turn heat to medium and simmer for 35 to 40 minutes, stirring often and gently, taking care not to mash the fruit slices, until contents are thick and shiny. Cool and store.

Yield: 6 pints (3 L)

Black Plum Chutney

I often use this chutney with roast poultry and meat. It is also a delicious topping for hors d'oeuvres, especially those that are pastry based.

Directions

In a medium saucepan, combine vinegar, wine, sugar, ginger, and spices with salt to taste. Simmer over low heat for 10 minutes. Add plums and reserved seeds. Cook over medium heat until chutney is thick and shiny, about 30 to 35 minutes. Remove seeds with a spoon and discard. Cool and store.

Yield: 1½ cups (375 ml)

1 cup (250 ml) apple cider vinegar

½ cup (125 ml) red wine

½ cup (125 ml) sugar

1 teaspoon (5 ml) grated ginger

1 teaspoon (5 ml) ground cinnamon

⅛ teaspoon (0.5 ml) ground nutmeg

Salt

6 black plums, trimmed and sliced, with a few seeds reserved

Peach Chutney

Pick ripe peaches that are still firm to the touch for this delicious chutney. It is my favorite accompaniment to a roast bird, roast leg of lamb, Thanksgiving turkey, or Christmas ham. The chutney also makes a delicious salad with goat cheese, honeyed walnuts, and greens dressed in a lemony vinaigrette.

Directions

Combine diced peaches, raisins, lemon juice, onion, ginger, cayenne pepper, and the rosemary sachet in a medium pan. Cook over high heat for 5 minutes, stirring constantly. Turn heat to medium, stir in sugar and vinegar, add salt to taste, and cook for 30 minutes. Remove and discard rosemary sachet. Continue cooking for 15 minutes until peaches turn translucent and chutney is thick and shiny. Cool and store.

Yield: 2 quarts (2 L)

4 large peaches, peeled, pitted, and diced (about 4 cups [1 L])

½ cup (125 ml) seedless golden raisins

½ cup (125 ml) lemon juice

½ cup (125 ml) minced onion

¼ cup (60 ml) minced ginger

1 teaspoon (5 ml) cayenne pepper

2 sprigs fresh rosemary, tied in a sachet

3 cups (750 ml) sugar

1 cup (250 ml) apple cider vinegar

Salt

Festive Fruit Chutney

½ cup (125 ml) white wine vinegar

1 cup (250 ml) balsamic vinegar

3 cups (500 ml) white wine

2 cups (500 ml) unsweetened pineapple juice

2 cups (500 ml) light brown sugar

1 Granny Smith apple, peeled, cored, and diced small

1 cup (250 ml) diced dried fruit (apricots, pears, figs)

1 cup (250 ml) diced winter melon preserve

½ cup (125 ml) chopped preserved cherries

½ cup (125 ml) diced ginger preserve

½ cup (125 ml) chopped almonds

½ cup (125 ml) chopped candied orange peel

Grated zest and juice of 1 orange

Grated zest and juice of 1 lemon

1 tablespoon (15 ml) ground cinnamon

½ teaspoon (2.5 ml) ground nutmeg

½ teaspoon (2.5 ml) ground mace

½ teaspoon (2.5 ml) ground cloves

1 teaspoon (5 ml) coarse ground black pepper

1 teaspoon (5 ml) ground cardamom

This chutney is always the star of the Christmas buffet. Winter melon and ginger preserves, which are readily available in Chinese grocery stores, add a unique taste and texture to the chutney. Dried fruit does not take as long to cook as fresh fruit and will retain its texture and add body to the chutney. Use a medium *rondeau* to cook the chutney, so there is enough space to stir often and easily without crushing the dried fruit.

Directions

Place vinegars, wine, pineapple juice, sugar, and apples in a medium *rondeau* and simmer over low heat for 10 minutes.

Add remaining ingredients and continue cooking over low heat for about 40 to 45 minutes, stirring frequently to prevent chutney from sticking. Cool and store.

Yield: 3 pints (1.5 L)

Date Chutney

This chutney is an uncommon yet refined accompaniment to meat and game. The recipe is a favorite, and I often serve it with grilled or roast lamb.

Directions

In a medium heavy-bottomed saucepan, cook lemon slices in water over low heat for about 30 minutes. Remove lemon slices, chop finely, and return to the saucepan.

Add apple cider vinegar, brown sugar, ginger, garlic, crushed red pepper, black pepper, mustard, and cinnamon and season with salt to taste. Simmer over low heat for 15 minutes, until syrup is fairly thick. Add dates and cashew nuts and continue to cook, stirring frequently, until chutney is thick and glazed, about 30 to 35 minutes. Cool and store.

Yield: 1 pint (500 ml)

2 lemons, sliced and seeds removed

2 cups (500 ml) water

1½ cups (375 ml) apple cider vinegar

2 cups (500 ml) brown sugar

2 tablespoons (30 ml) minced ginger

2 tablespoons (30 ml) minced garlic

1 tablespoon (15 ml) crushed red pepper

1 teaspoon (5 ml) coarse ground black pepper

1 tablespoon (15 ml) Dijon grainy mustard

1 teaspoon (5 ml) ground cinnamon

Salt

1 pound (453 g) seeded dates, diced small

½ cup (125 ml) coarsely chopped cashew nuts

Tamarind and Raisin Chutney

½ cup (125 ml) tamarind pulp

1½ to 2 cups (375 to 500 ml) hot water

1 to 1½ cups (250 to 375 ml) sugar,
or more to taste

1 teaspoon (5 ml) cayenne pepper

½ cup (125 ml) seedless raisins, coarsely
chopped

2 teaspoons (10 ml) dried ginger powder

Salt

2 teaspoons (10 ml) cumin seeds

The tree commonly known as tamarind is native to India and also grows profusely in Sri Lanka. Throughout Asia, both the pods and the leaves of the tamarind are valued for their medicinal properties. In flavor, tamarind is naturally fruity, slightly sweet, and very sour. Both children and adults love eating raw tamarind pods and leaves.

The sugar in this recipe brings out tamarind's flavor contrasts, and raisins intensify its sweet flavor. It is important to taste the mixture before it is cooked so that you can add more sugar or water as needed. Use this chutney when sauces with a sweet and sour note are called for. It is a standard dip for crispy samosas.

Directions

Combine tamarind pulp and water in a saucepan. Stir in sugar, taste and check for a good balance of sour and sweet, and add more sugar if needed. Add cayenne pepper, raisins, and ginger powder and season with salt to taste. Set aside.

In a small frying pan, roast cumin seeds to a dark color. Place seeds on a cutting board and crush them coarsely by running a rolling pin over them two or three times. Add to the saucepan and simmer over low heat for 30 minutes, until the mixture is syrupy and glistening and coats the back of a spoon. Cool and place in a jar. Cover jar and refrigerate.

Yield: 1 pint (500 ml)

Cranberry and Orange Chutney

1½ pounds (680 g) cranberries, fresh or frozen

1½ pounds (680 g) granulated sugar

2 cups (500 ml) orange juice

2 tablespoons (30 ml) grated orange zest

2 teaspoons (10 ml) ground cinnamon

1 teaspoon (5 ml) ground cloves

2 teaspoons (10 ml) dried ginger powder

Cranberries have a thick red skin, a firm texture, and a very tart flavor. It must be noted that the berries do not all taste the same; some are highly acidic. As a rule, I start with equal amounts of sugar and berries. As soon as the sugar has melted and the berries are almost ready to pop open, I do a taste test and, more often than not, find it needs a little more sugar. Whether you call it a chutney or a sauce, it is delicious. Serve as tradition dictates with roast turkey and roast game birds.

Directions

Pick through cranberries and discard soft or bruised berries. Wash and drain well in a colander.

Combine sugar and remaining ingredients in a medium heavy-bottomed saucepan and bring to a slow simmer. Add cranberries and cook over medium heat for about 15 minutes or until cranberries begin to burst. Taste mixture for sweetness and stir in more sugar if needed. With a ladle, skim and discard the foam that forms on top, so the chutney will be clear and shiny. Simmer for 5 more minutes. Cool and store.

Yield: 2 quarts (2 L)

Dried Cranberry Chutney

Dried cranberry chutney looks luscious, with its shiny burgundy color. Red wine, red wine vinegar, and red onion make up the base that gives the chutney its good looks. The fruit-friendly spices cinnamon and cloves enliven the chutney, which is a favorite on the holiday table. Apart from its traditional uses, it partners well with cooked grains such as quinoa.

Directions

Combine all ingredients and a pinch of salt in a heavy-bottomed medium pan. Place pan over low heat and simmer about 1 hour, stirring often, until chutney looks glazed. Discard cinnamon stick and bay leaf. Cool and store.

Yield: 2 cups (500 ml)

8 ounces (226 g) dried cranberries

1 cup (250 ml) sugar, or to taste

1 cup (250 ml) red wine

½ cup (125 ml) red wine vinegar

Juice of 1 orange

Juice of 1 lemon

1 tablespoon (15 ml) grated orange zest

½ cup (125 ml) finely chopped red onion

1 tablespoon (15 ml) finely chopped ginger

½ teaspoon (2.5 ml) crushed red pepper

½ teaspoon (2.5 ml) ground cloves

2-inch (5 cm) piece of cinnamon stick

1 bay leaf

Salt

Wi Apple Chutney

15 mature but unripe wi apples, peeled and trimmed

¼ cup (60 ml) golden raisins

2 cups (500 ml) apple cider vinegar

2 cups (500 ml) sugar

1 tablespoon (15 ml) chopped garlic

1 tablespoon (15 ml) chopped ginger

1 tablespoon (15 ml) chopped onion

2-inch (5 cm) piece of cinnamon stick

1 tablespoon (15 ml) ground black mustard seeds

1 tablespoon (15 ml) crushed red pepper

1 teaspoon (5 ml) ground cloves

Salt to taste

The wi apple is a plum-shaped fruit with firm, pale, crunchy flesh. It is best for chutney when the fruits are mature but not yet ripe. The spiny seeds, which can bruise the mouth, are the fruit's distinguishing feature. The nearly ripe fruit, whole with its seeds, is good in preserves (see **Wi Apple Preserve,** p. 219).

Directions

Quarter the apples lengthwise and remove and discard seeds. Slice into ¾-inch (1.8 cm) slices. (You will need about 2 cups [500 ml].) Place apples and remaining ingredients in a medium heavy-bottomed pan. Simmer over low heat for about 1½ hours, until chutney is thick and shiny, stirring often to avoid scorching. Cool and store.

Yield: 1½ cups (375 ml)

Hot Lime Pickles Chutney

1 pound (453 g) **Hot and Spicy Lime Pickles** (p. 101)

½ pound (226 g) golden seedless raisins

10 dried red chilies, stems removed

1 tablespoon (15 ml) black mustard seeds

1 tablespoon (15 ml) minced ginger

1 tablespoon (15 ml) minced garlic

3 cups (725 ml) apple cider vinegar

2 cups (500 ml) sugar

4-inch (10 cm) piece of cinnamon stick

This is a favorite among chutney lovers. It does wonders for a very simple meal of rice and curry and also complements rich rice dishes such as buriyani and rice pilaf.

Directions

Cut lime pickles into thin strips, discarding any seeds. Place in a medium bowl and add raisins, mixing to blend.

In a blender, puree chilies, black mustard seeds, ginger, and garlic with 1 cup of the vinegar until mixture is a smooth consistency.

Place remaining 2 cups of vinegar, sugar, and cinnamon stick in a medium pan. Add pureed ingredients, stir well, and bring to a slow simmer. Cook until syrup is fairly thick. Remove from heat.

When syrup is cool, add it to the bowl of pickled limes and raisins. Mix well. Cool and store.

Yield: 2 pints (1 L)

Gooseberry Chutney

4 cups (1 L) gooseberries

1 cup (250 ml) water

1 tablespoon (15 ml) vegetable oil

¼ teaspoon (1.25 ml) fenugreek seeds

¼ teaspoon (1.25 ml) cumin seeds

½ teaspoon (2.5 ml) black mustard seeds

3 garlic cloves, thinly sliced

1-inch (2.5 cm) piece of ginger, julienned

2-inch (5 cm) piece of cinnamon stick

1 small bay leaf

¾ cup (180 ml) distilled vinegar

About 2 cups (500 ml) sugar, or to taste

Salt

Here in Hawai'i, a friend who had a purple variety of gooseberry in her garden supplied me with the berries when they were in season. I give fragrance to this chutney with a mix of whole spices fried in oil, as they do in India, and balance the highly acidic fruit with sugar. As the chutney starts to cook, taste and add more sugar if needed.

Directions

Place gooseberries and water in a medium saucepan and cook over medium heat until berries are soft, about 8 minutes. Press berries through a sieve and discard seeds and skins. Reserve berry puree.

Heat oil in a small saucepan, then add fenugreek seeds, cumin seeds, and black mustard seeds and cook a few seconds over moderate heat until seeds start to pop (this takes only a few seconds). Add garlic and ginger and cook a few more seconds. Fold in gooseberry puree and add cinnamon stick, bay leaf, vinegar, and sugar. Season with salt to taste. Simmer over medium heat until chutney is shiny, about 35 to 40 minutes. It will be runny when done. Remove and discard cinnamon stick and bay leaf. Cool and store.

Yield: 1 pint (500 ml)

Pear and Ginger Chutney

This chutney makes a tasty topping for ice cream. It is also good with a fresh spinach and goat cheese salad dressed with a light vinaigrette or paired with shaved Parmesan on a lightly dressed arugula salad.

8 pears (about 1½ pounds [680 g])

½ cup (125 ml) coarsely grated ginger

1 cup (250 ml) apple juice

1½ cups (375 ml) sugar

1 cup (250 ml) apple cider vinegar

¼ cup (60 ml) lemon juice

¼ cup (60 ml) grated lemon zest

1 teaspoon (5 ml) ground cinnamon

¼ teaspoon (1.25 ml) grated nutmeg

½ teaspoon (2.5 ml) salt, or to taste

Directions

Peel and core pears. Cut into ¼-inch (0.6 cm) cubes and set aside.

Combine the remaining ingredients in a medium saucepan. Place over high heat and cook for 10 minutes. Add cubed pears and cook, stirring to prevent scorching, until pears turn translucent and are glazed, about 30 to 40 minutes. Cool and store.

Yield: 3 cups (750 ml)

Papaya Chutney

This gorgeous chutney is in between a chutney and a jam. It is mildly spiced, and the white wine vinegar and citrus zest give it a very rounded, refined taste.

1 pound (453 g) half-ripe papayas, peeled, quartered, and seeded

1 tablespoon (15 ml) coarsely shredded ginger

½ teaspoon (2.5 ml) ground allspice

1 teaspoon (5 ml) ground cardamom seeds

½ teaspoon (2.5 ml) black pepper

½ cup (125 ml) distilled vinegar

¾ cup (180 ml) sugar, or to taste

1 tablespoon (15 ml) grated orange zest

4 ounces (120 ml) orange juice

1 tablespoon (15 ml) grated lemon zest

1 tablespoon (15 ml) fresh lemon juice

Salt

Directions

Cut papayas into ¼-inch (0.6 cm) cubes. Place papaya and remaining ingredients in a small heavy-bottomed pan, season with salt to taste, and bring to a slow simmer over low heat. Simmer until mixture coats the back of a spoon. Cool and store.

Yield: 1 pint (500 ml)

Tomato and Lemon Chutney

Tomato and lemon are two colorful partners and bring out the best in each other. In this recipe, I use whole spices: fried in oil, they lend texture and a lingering aroma to this elegant chutney. Roma tomatoes, which have very few seeds, work better than regular tomatoes in this recipe. The chutney is an obvious partner for seafood: I serve it with spicy shrimp, an appetizer that is a hit with guests.

Directions

Add oil to a medium heavy-bottomed sauté pan and place over medium heat. When oil is hot, add cinnamon stick, cumin, fenugreek, and black mustard seeds. With a spoon, stir spices around, and when mustard seeds start to pop (this takes only a few seconds), add crushed red pepper, garlic, and ginger. Stir and cook a few seconds, then stir in sugar and vinegar. Stir in tomatoes, season with salt to taste, and cook for 40 minutes. Stir occasionally, to keep chutney from sticking to the bottom of the pan, and gently, to avoid crushing the tomatoes. Fold in lemon zest and cook 10 minutes until chutney is glazed. Cool and store.

Yield: 2 cups (500 ml)

2 tablespoons (30 ml) vegetable oil

2-inch (5 m) piece of cinnamon stick

¼ teaspoon (1.25 ml) whole cumin seeds

¼ teaspoon (1.25 ml) fenugreek seeds

½ teaspoon (2.5 ml) black mustard seeds

¼ teaspoon (1.25 ml) crushed red pepper

4 garlic cloves, thinly sliced

1 tablespoon (5 ml) thinly shredded ginger

½ cup (125 ml) sugar, or to taste

¾ cup (180 ml) white wine vinegar

1½ pounds (680 g) Roma tomatoes, diced small

Salt

Zest of 1 lemon, julienned

Green Tomato Chutney

1½ pounds (680 g) green tomatoes

1 tablespoon (15 ml) vegetable oil

½ teaspoon (2.5 ml) cumin seeds

½ teaspoon (2.5 ml) black mustard seeds

10 fresh curry leaves (optional)

½ cup (125 ml) finely chopped onion

2 tablespoons (30 ml) grated ginger

2 tablespoons (30 ml) chopped garlic

⅛ teaspoon (0.6 ml) turmeric

1 teaspoon (5 ml) crushed red pepper

1½ cups (375 ml) sugar

Juice of 1 lemon

¾ cup (180 ml) distilled vinegar

Salt

This is an all-purpose chutney, easy to make. It is a vegetarian's delight. The curry leaves, if you include them, contribute an exotic look.

Directions

Slice green tomatoes and set aside.

Heat oil in a medium saucepan over medium heat, then stir in cumin seeds and black mustard seeds. When mustard seeds start to pop (this takes only a few seconds), add curry leaves (if using), onion, ginger, and garlic and continue stirring until onions turn translucent. Add turmeric, crushed red pepper, sugar, lemon juice, and vinegar with salt to taste and bring to a slow simmer. Stir in tomatoes and cook over medium heat until chutney is thick and shiny, about 30 to 35 minutes. Cool and refrigerate.

Yield: 1½ cups (375 ml)

Green Tomato and Apricot Chutney

2 tablespoons (30 ml) vegetable oil

2-inch (5 cm) piece of cinnamon stick

½ teaspoon (2.5 ml) black mustard seeds

½ teaspoon (2.5 ml) crushed red pepper

4 garlic cloves, thinly sliced

1 tablespoon (15 ml) thinly shredded ginger

½ cup (125 ml) sugar

½ cup (125 ml) apple cider vinegar

1½ pounds (680 g) green tomatoes, diced small

2 apricots, seeded and diced small

Salt

Chutneys made with green tomatoes and any fruit are best with seafood.

Directions

Add oil to a medium pan and place over medium heat. When oil is hot, add cinnamon stick and mustard seeds. With a spoon, stir spices around, and when mustard seeds start to pop (this takes only a few seconds), add crushed red pepper, garlic, and ginger. Stir and cook a few seconds, then mix in sugar and vinegar. Stir in tomatoes and apricots, season with salt to taste, and cook for 45 minutes, stirring occasionally to keep chutney from sticking to the bottom of the pan. Cook until chutney is glazed. Cool and store.

Yield: 2 cups (500 ml)

Kabocha Chutney

Kabocha pumpkin is a sweet pumpkin and makes a good chutney. This accompaniment is a fine addition to the Thanksgiving menu.

Directions

Cut pumpkin into large dice. In a medium pot, add water and 1 teaspoon (5 ml) salt and place over medium heat. Bring to a boil, then carefully add pumpkin and cook until tender, about 8 to 10 minutes.

Drain pumpkin in a colander, transfer pieces to a large bowl, and mash to a coarse pulp. Weigh mashed pumpkin, add raisins and walnuts, and set aside.

Place remaining ingredients in a medium saucepan, bring to a simmer, and cook over low heat until the mixture is slightly thickened, about 10 minutes. Stir in pumpkin mixture. Continue cooking, about 30 to 40 minutes, stirring constantly to prevent scorching. Cool and store.

Yield: 1 pint (500 ml)

1½ pounds (681 g) kabocha or other sweet pumpkin, peeled and seeded (about 1 pound [454 g])

3 cups (725 ml) cold water

Salt

½ cup (125 ml) golden raisins

¼ cup (60 ml) chopped walnuts

Brown sugar, same weight as the weight of cooked pumpkin

1 teaspoon (5 ml) cayenne pepper

2 teaspoons (10 ml) ground cinnamon

½ teaspoon (2.5 ml) nutmeg

2 teaspoons (10 ml) minced ginger

2 teaspoons (10 ml) minced garlic

½ lemon, seeds removed and chopped fine

1½ cups (375 ml) apple cider vinegar

½ cup (125 ml) maple syrup

FRUIT "CHAAT MASALA"

HAWAIIAN CHILI PEPPER WATER

BLACK BEAN SALSA

BLACK BEAN, MANGO,
AND PINEAPPLE SALSA

THREE RELISHES FOR CHIPS:
SPINACH AND SOUR CREAM RELISH;
SWEET AND SOUR BEET RELISH;
CARROT, ORANGE, AND MINT RELISH

GUACAMOLE

PAPAYA SALSA

SWEET MANGO RELISH

FRESH APPLE RELISH

MOUNTAIN APPLE RELISH

HOT GREEN CILANTRO RELISH

BANANA RELISH

POMEGRANATE RELISH

RICE WITH CHICKPEAS, RAISINS,
AND CASHEW NUTS

FRIED EGGPLANT AND YOGURT RELISH

EGGPLANT RELISH

BABA GHANOUSH

HUMMUS

ORANGE AND DATE RELISH

GRATED CARROT, ORANGE,
AND RAISIN RELISH

MUNG BEAN AND COCONUT RELISH

COCONUT RELISH

MANGO AND COCONUT RELISH

CUCUMBERS IN YOGURT

CUCUMBER, ONION, AND TOMATO RELISH

BENGALI SPICY TOMATO "PACHADI"

CHARRED TOMATO RELISH

HAWAIIAN LOMILOMI SALMON

SALTED SALMON

HAWAIIAN FRIED "HAUPIA"

HERB PESTO

PESTO

MINTY CASHEW PESTO

MINT AND COCONUT RELISH

ROASTED GARLIC WITH HONEY
AND BALSAMIC VINEGAR

SPICED DAL "ON THE SIDE"

TOMATO RELISH FOR FRIED OKRA

EGGPLANT RAITA

POTATOES WITH CUCUMBER
AND YOGURT DRESSING

CUCUMBER RELISH WITH
COCONUT MILK DRESSING

POMELO RELISH

OGO RELISH

ORANGE, FENNEL, AND
RED ONION RELISH

BRANDADE

BLOOD ORANGE AND MINT RELISH

SICILIAN HOT RELISH

HARISSA

TAPENADE

TOMATO RELISH WITH GOAT CHEESE

CHERMOULA

FRESH CORIANDER RELISH

ROUILLE

CHARRED BUTTERNUT SQUASH
AND TOMATO RELISH

DILL RAITA

SPINACH RAITA

SPICED YOGURT

RELISHES

Relishes are pickled, cooked or uncooked preparations made with mainly vegetables, fruit, and dairy products. Sometimes seafood and meat are also used. Relishes are also referred to as condiments. They are very different from typical Western relishes such as hot dog relish and piccalilli. They use aromatic herbs such as mint, coriander, curry leaves, basil, and ripe and unripe fruit such as green mango and vegetables such as tomatoes, eggplant, and spinach, to name a few. Green chilies, fresh herbs, garlic, shallots, onions, lime or lemon juice, and tamarind are used to enhance flavor. Grated fresh coconut and yogurt are common ingredients in relishes. They contribute a creamy luscious flavor, offset heat in some dishes, and add to the overall taste of others.

Exotic spices, such as ground asafetida and black mustard seeds, are fried in oil and add fragrance and intrigue to **Coconut Relish** (p. 51). Relishes may be smooth, pasty, crunchy, or crispy. Some are sauce-like preparations most often served on the side or as dips and spreads, as small salads and substitutes for sauces, as glazes on roasts, or as simple taste enhancers. Some relishes are cooling and counteract the heat and spiciness of their partner foods. Many others with assertive flavors add extra kick and enliven dishes.

Relishes from around the world have their own unique qualities. Some are a necessary component of a dish, not just an accompaniment. For example, dosa, a rice and dal pancake that is a favorite in India and Sri Lanka, is always served with a saucy coconut relish. A chutni is an uncooked relish and is popular in India, Sri Lanka, and other Asian countries. Many people love these taste enhancers. **Hot Green Cilantro Relish** (p. 37) is a spicy chutni; **Banana Relish** (p. 38) is a sweet and creamy chutni. Both are examples of the traditional relishes of South Asia, especially India. Every culture has its own favorites. Thus, relishes cover a whole spectrum of tastes: sweet, sour, umami, salty, and bitter.

Today, relishes are used in a myriad of innovative ways around the world. They are at their best when freshly made and should be consumed quickly. Use only nonreactive utensils, equipment, and containers for preparing, serving, and storing relishes. Certain relishes should be refrigerated, yet even then, they become discolored and lose their aroma after a day or two.

Fruit "Chaat Masala"

This dish makes a wonderful small starter. The masala I use in the recipe gives an enticing aroma and pungency to the fruit and will awaken the taste buds of those who await the main dish. Use any fruit that you have on hand.

Directions

Arrange sliced fruit on plates and sprinkle pomegranate seeds decoratively on top. Chill. Sprinkle a little chaat masala on sliced fruit just before serving.

6 servings

1 ripe mango, peeled and sliced

1 papaya, peeled, seeded, and sliced

½ pineapple, peeled, halved lengthwise, cored, and sliced

½ cup (125 ml) fresh pomegranate seeds

3 tablespoons (45 ml) **Chaat Masala** (see Blended Spices p. 227)

Hawaiian Chili Pepper Water

Hawaiian chili pepper water is a table condiment. It is so popular that some restaurants always have it on the table. Bird's eye chilies are best for this recipe. Always pick red, plump chilies. Some varieties of bird's eye chilies are green and yellow.

Directions

Use a sterilized quart-size narrow-mouthed bottle with a lid. Add chilies, garlic, salt, and water. Put the lid on the bottle and shake well. Leave out overnight.

The next day, shake the bottle and then refrigerate. Let sit for 2 to 3 days before using. When the chili pepper water runs low, you may replenish with more water. Chili pepper water keeps for 3 months.

Yield: 1 quart (1 L)

1 cup (250 ml) chilies with stems attached, washed

1 garlic clove, crushed

Hawaiian salt to taste

2 cups (500 ml) cold water

Black Bean Salsa

1½ cups (375 ml) cooked black beans

½ small red onion, diced small

3 plum tomatoes, diced small

¼ cup (60 ml) tomato sauce

2 tablespoons (30 ml) coarsely chopped cilantro

1 tablespoon (15 ml) lemon juice

1 tablespoon (15 ml) white wine vinegar

2 jalapeños, halved lengthwise, seeded, and sliced

2 fresh red chilies, sliced lengthwise, seeded, and sliced

1 teaspoon (5 ml) black pepper

2 tablespoons (30 ml) olive oil

Salt

This superb accompaniment for barbecued meat is easy to put together. The fresh plum tomatoes give the salsa a vibrant taste, and the tomato sauce adds body.

Directions

Combine all ingredients except olive oil in a large bowl and add salt to taste. Mix well and fold in olive oil. Refrigerate and transfer to a medium salad bowl and serve cold.

Yield: 1 pint (500 ml)

Black Bean, Mango, and Pineapple Salsa

1½ cups (375 ml) cooked black beans

½ cup (125 ml) small-diced ripe mango

½ cup (125 ml) small-diced pineapple

½ cup (125 ml) small-diced red onion

½ cup (125 ml) small-diced red bell pepper

½ cup (125 ml) chopped cilantro

2 jalapeños, seeded and chopped

1 tablespoon (15 ml) minced ginger

2 teaspoons (10 ml) ground cumin

2 teaspoons (10 ml) black pepper

½ cup (125 ml) lime juice

2 tablespoons (30 ml) olive oil

Salt

This salsa is a popular picnic dish and a delightful accompaniment to barbecued meat. Apple and papaya are good substitutes for mango and pineapple.

Directions

In a large bowl, combine all ingredients except olive oil and add salt to taste. Mix well and fold in olive oil. Refrigerate. Transfer to a medium salad bowl and serve cold.

8 to 10 servings

Three Relishes for Chips

The following three relishes are simple and delicious and take almost no time to prepare. There are many uses for these relishes. Served with a platter of chips, they would be a wonderful starter for a crowd. For an attractive presentation, serve these relishes in small glass bowls.

SPINACH AND SOUR CREAM RELISH

Directions

Squeeze excess liquid out of spinach, then chop fine. Set aside.

In a small bowl, whisk sour cream, mayonnaise, Parmesan cheese, hot sauce, garlic, and black pepper until smooth. Season lightly with salt to taste and fold in dill and spinach. Spoon into a small serving bowl.

Yield: 1½ cups (375 ml)

½ cup (125 ml) cooked fresh or frozen spinach
¾ cup (180 ml) sour cream
1 tablespoon (15 ml) mayonnaise
1 tablespoon (15 ml) grated Parmesan cheese
½ teaspoon (2.5 ml) hot sauce
1 teaspoon (5 ml) minced garlic
¼ teaspoon (1.25 ml) black pepper
Salt
1 tablespoon (15 ml) chopped dill

SWEET AND SOUR BEET RELISH

Directions

Place grated beets in a bowl and set aside.

In a small nonreactive pan, combine cider vinegar, orange juice, and sugar. Cook over medium heat until reduced by half.

Pour mixture on beets, add coriander seeds and black pepper, season lightly with salt to taste, and toss to combine. Spoon relish into a small glass bowl and sprinkle with chopped parsley.

Yield: 1½ cups (375 ml)

1 cup (250 ml) peeled, coarsely grated raw beets
1 tablespoon (15 ml) apple cider vinegar
½ cup (125 ml) orange juice
2 teaspoons (10 ml) sugar
½ teaspoon (2.5 ml) finely crushed coriander seeds
1 teaspoon (5 ml) black pepper
Salt
1 tablespoon (15 ml) chopped parsley

CARROT, ORANGE, AND MINT RELISH

Directions

Place all ingredients in a bowl. Season lightly with salt to taste and mix gently to combine. Spoon into a small glass bowl.

Yield: 1½ cups (375 ml)

1 cup (250 ml) peeled, coarsely grated carrots
¼ cup (60 m) orange juice
¼ cup (60 ml) orange segments
1 tablespoon (15 ml) lemon juice
1 tablespoon (15 ml) shredded mint leaves
1 teaspoon (5 ml) ground cumin
2 teaspoons (10 m) honey
Salt

Guacamole

5 avocados, halved, pitted, and peeled

½ cup (125 ml) thinly sliced green onion

1 jalapeño, seeded and minced

½ cup (125 ml) finely chopped cilantro

1 teaspoon (5 ml) black pepper

2 teaspoons (10 ml) Tabasco sauce

Juice of 2 limes

Salt

This dip is best with its usual partner, a basket of crisp tortilla chips. Or try it on crostini and crackers for a change of pace.

Directions

Coarsely chop avocado and place in a ceramic bowl. Add green onion, jalapeño, cilantro, black pepper, Tabasco sauce, and lime juice. Add salt to taste. Use a heavy wooden spoon to crush ingredients and mix thoroughly until flavors are blended.

Yield: 2 cups (500 ml)

Papaya Salsa

1 medium ripe papaya

1 fresh red chili, seeded and finely chopped

1 green chili, seeded and finely chopped

¼ cup (60 ml) finely chopped red onion

1 teaspoon (5 ml) grated ginger

1 tablespoon (15 ml) thinly sliced green onion

¼ cup (60 ml) chopped cilantro

Juice of ½ orange

Juice of 2 limes

1 teaspoon (5 ml) sugar

1 teaspoon (5 ml) black pepper

Salt

Just-ripe, soft-to-the-touch papaya is essential to this relish. Over-ripe papaya loses its shape when it is diced and combined with the other ingredients. The salsa is a good accompaniment to roast poultry or pork and may also be served on its own with a basket of chips.

Directions

Halve papaya. Seed, peel, dice small, and place in a dish. Add remaining ingredients and season with salt to taste. Toss and chill.

6 to 8 servings

Sweet Mango Relish

This is a good starter for an elegant dinner. Serve it in small portions. Toss the relish just before you serve, so the vegetables stay crisp.

Directions

Place mangoes, vegetables, and herbs in a bowl.

In a separate bowl, whisk together chili paste, honey, lime juice, fish sauce, and dried shrimp and season with salt to taste. Pour over mangoes and vegetables. Toss gently to combine the flavors. Spoon into individual serving dishes and sprinkle with peanuts and garlic flakes.

6 to 8 servings

2 to 3 peeled, thinly sliced, ripe mangoes (2 cups [500 ml])

¼ cup (60 ml) julienned red onion

2 green chilies, chopped

¼ cup (60 ml) julienned carrots

¼ cup (60 ml) julienned cabbage

½ cup (125 ml) sliced mint leaves

½ cup (125 ml) cilantro leaves

2 teaspoons (10 ml) chili paste

1 tablespoon (15 ml) honey, or more to taste

Juice of 2 large limes

1 tablespoon (15 ml) fish sauce

1 tablespoon (15 ml) dried shrimp, roasted and finely crushed

Salt

2 tablespoons (30 ml) finely chopped roasted peanuts

1 tablespoon (15 ml) garlic flakes

Fresh Apple Relish

Apple relish is easy to assemble, and small portions make a great starter to a meal. It is versatile and may be served as a salad or as a delicious snack on a hot afternoon.

Directions

Place diced apples in a bowl of acidulated water (water mixed with a small amount of lemon juice or vinegar), to prevent discoloration, and set aside. When ready to assemble relish, drain apples in a strainer and wipe dry with paper towels.

In a bowl, combine apples with the rest of the ingredients and season with salt to taste. Toss to combine flavors. Serve chilled.

6 servings

2 Granny Smith apples, peeled, cored, and diced small

½ cup (125 ml) grated fresh coconut

1 tablespoon (15 ml) chopped almonds

2 tablespoons (30 ml) finely chopped onion

1 tablespoon (15 ml) finely chopped green chili

1 tablespoon (15 ml) finely chopped fresh red chili

¼ teaspoon (1.25 ml) cayenne pepper

1 teaspoon (5 ml) black pepper

¼ cup (60 ml) lemon juice

Salt

Mountain Apple Relish

In Hawai'i, many varieties of mountain apple are abundant during summer months. The fruit is juicy but not very sweet. My favorite way to enjoy mountain apples is to dip them whole in a mixture of vinegar, sugar, hot chili, and salt. It is a perfect balance of taste. This deep red Hawaiian mountain apple is lovely—seedless, sweet, and juicy. It makes a delicious salad.

10 mountain apples

¼ cup (60 ml) diced red onion

¼ cup (60 ml) shredded mint leaves

1 teaspoon (5 ml) chili paste

½ teaspoon (2.5 ml) black pepper

2 teaspoons (10 ml) Dijon grainy mustard

¼ cup (60 ml) white wine vinegar

Salt

3 teaspoons (15 ml) sugar

Directions

Slice mountain apples lengthwise about ⅛ inch (0.3 cm) thick and place in a medium bowl. Add onion and mint.

In a small bowl, whisk remaining ingredients with salt and sugar to taste and set aside. When ready to serve, pour over fruit mixture and toss gently to mix. Transfer to a small serving dish.

6 servings

Hot Green Cilantro Relish

Cilantro relish is easy to put together. It is a common accompaniment to Indian breads and makes a tasty sauce for grilled seafood. As with other fresh relishes, this relish should be served immediately after preparation.

1 cup (250 ml) cilantro leaves

½ cup (125 ml) chopped onion

4 green chilies, chopped

2 fresh red chilies, chopped

1 tablespoon (15 ml) chopped ginger

2 medium tomatoes, chopped

Juice of 1 lemon

1 teaspoon (5 ml) tamarind juice

½ cup (125 ml) water

Salt

Directions

Place ingredients in a blender and puree until smooth. Season with salt to taste. Transfer to a small serving dish.

4 servings

Banana Relish

1 cup (250 ml) large-diced ripe bananas

2 tablespoons (30 ml) lemon juice

1 tablespoon (15 ml) melted unsalted butter

½ teaspoon (2.5 ml) cayenne pepper

Salt

½ cup (125 ml) grated fresh coconut

2 teaspoons (10 ml) **Chaat Masala** (p. 227)

Everybody, from children to grown-ups, loves this relish. It takes only a few minutes to put together. But be careful with the salt—it needs only a big pinch or none at all.

Directions

In a bowl, toss bananas in lemon juice, butter, and cayenne pepper and add salt to taste. Sprinkle coconut over bananas and toss to combine all. Chill.

Transfer bananas to a small dish and sprinkle with chaat masala when ready to serve.

Yield: 1½ cups (375 ml)

Pomegranate Relish

Pomegranates date back to the time of the Dravidians in India. King Solomon is believed to have had them growing in his orchards. Sanskrit literature often refers to the beauty of pomegranate flowers and seeds. In India and Sri Lanka, pomegranate is valued for the medicinal properties of its skin and seeds. Juicy, plump pomegranates are now available in most cities around the world. Lately, fresh pomegranate seeds have become a popular addition to salads.

Directions

Combine pomegranate seeds, tomatoes, and radicchio in a medium bowl.

Heat olive oil in a small sauté pan over medium heat. Add onions and cook until they turn a light golden color. Stir in garlic and cook a few seconds, then add the contents of the pan to the pomegranate seeds and vegetables in the bowl.

For the dressing, combine balsamic vinegar, molasses, lemon juice, crushed red pepper, and black pepper in a small bowl. Whisk well. Pour over pomegranate seeds and vegetables and toss gently to combine flavors. Season with a pinch of salt (keeping in mind that feta cheese is salty). Spoon into a medium salad bowl and sprinkle with feta cheese and mint.

6 to 8 servings

1 cup (250 ml) pomegranate seeds

1 cup (250 ml) sliced plum tomatoes

½ cup (125 ml) sliced radicchio

1 tablespoon (15 ml) olive oil

1 cup (250 ml) sliced red onion

1 tablespoon (15 ml) minced garlic

1 tablespoon (15 ml) balsamic vinegar

1 tablespoon (15 ml) pomegranate molasses

¼ cup (60 ml) lemon juice

1 tablespoon (15 ml) crushed red pepper

1 teaspoon (5 ml) black pepper

Salt

¼ cup (60 ml) crumbled feta cheese

½ cup (125 ml) sliced mint leaves

Rice with Chickpeas, Raisins, and Cashew Nuts

1 cup (250 ml) cooked black rice or grain of your choice

1 cup (250 ml) cooked basmati rice

1 teaspoon (5 ml) black pepper

Salt

½ cup (125 ml) melted unsalted butter

¼ cup (60 ml) olive oil

¼ cup (60 ml) cashew nuts

¼ cup (60 ml) golden raisins

¼ cup (60 ml) dried cranberries

1 small onion, thinly sliced

2 green chilies, thinly sliced

1 tablespoon (15 ml) flour

2-inch (5 cm) piece of cinnamon stick

1 tablespoon (15 ml) curry powder

1 cup (250 ml) cooked chickpeas (garbanzo beans)

1 teaspoon (5 ml) ground cumin seeds

½ cup (125 ml) mint leaves

This rice dish is an excellent vehicle for accompaniments such as poppadum, chutney, and yogurt-based relishes. Cooked black rice tastes like toasted nuts, and the shiny grains give the dish an elegant appearance. Black rice is hardy and needs to be soaked before cooking. Follow the instructions on the package.

Directions

In a bowl, combine cooked black rice and cooked basmati rice. Season with black pepper, add salt to taste, fold in melted butter, and set aside.

Heat olive oil in a pan over moderate heat. Fry cashews to a light golden color, transfer to a small bowl, and set aside. Turn off heat to lower the oil temperature, add raisins and cranberries to the pan, and fry for 2 to 3 seconds, just enough to plump them, then add to the cashews. (Reserve the frying pan and cooking oil after removing raisins and cranberries.)

Toss onion and green chili slices in flour, shaking off excess. Using the reserved frying pan and oil, add floured onion and green chili slices and fry until crisp. Remove and add to cashews, raisins, and cranberries in the bowl.

There should be about a tablespoon of oil left in the pan. Turn heat to low and add cinnamon stick and curry powder. Cook, stirring to mix, for 1 minute. Toss chickpeas in the ground cumin and add to the pan. Cook, stirring to mix, for 4 to 5 minutes. Fold in seasoned rice and cook for 2 to 3 minutes. Remove from heat. Cover the pan and let sit for 5 minutes.

Spoon rice and chickpeas into a dish. Fold in fried cashews, raisins, cranberries, onion, and green chilies. Serve in a medium bowl and sprinkle with mint leaves.

6 servings

Fried Eggplant and Yogurt Relish

Many people love eggplant, and this relish seasoned with yogurt is a favorite among vegetarians. You may also serve it as a side dish with fish and poultry.

Directions

Trim ends of eggplant and cut into ¼-inch (0.6 cm) slices. Place in a bowl, sprinkle with 1 teaspoon (5 ml) salt, and set aside for 15 minutes. Transfer eggplant to a colander, rinse, and wipe dry. Place in a clean bowl, add turmeric, and mix well to coat.

Heat oil in a skillet or sauté pan over high heat and fry eggplant in batches to a golden brown. Place each batch on paper towels to drain.

In another sauté pan, add 1 tablespoon (15 ml) of the oil used to fry the eggplant and place over medium heat. Add onions and cook for 3 to 4 minutes until onions are lightly browned. Add green and red chilies and garlic and fry until garlic is a light golden color. Turn heat to low and stir in spices. Cook a few seconds, fold in fried eggplant, and immediately remove pan from heat.

Transfer to a dish and cool. Stir in yogurt. Serve at room temperature.

6 to 8 servings

4 long eggplants

Salt

½ teaspoon (2.5 ml) turmeric

½ cup (125 ml) vegetable oil

1 small onion, cut lengthwise into ¼-inch (0.6 cm) slices

3 fresh green chilies, sliced

3 fresh red chilies, sliced

1 tablespoon (15 ml) sliced garlic

1 teaspoon (5 ml) coarse ground black pepper

1 teaspoon (5 ml) roasted ground fennel seeds

1 teaspoon (5 ml) black mustard seeds, coarsely ground

1 cup (250 ml) yogurt, whisked smooth

Eggplant Relish

4 long eggplants

Salt

¼ teaspoon (1.25 ml) turmeric

Vegetable oil for frying

1 small onion, thinly sliced

2 green chilies, thinly sliced

1 teaspoon (5 ml) minced garlic

1 teaspoon (5 ml) ground coriander

1 teaspoon (5 ml) ground cumin

1 teaspoon (5 ml) cayenne pepper

1 tablespoon (15 ml) Dijon grainy mustard

2 tablespoons (30 ml) apple cider vinegar

1 teaspoon (5 ml) sugar

¼ cup (60 ml) coconut milk

Eggplant relish has been a favorite accompaniment to rice and curry meals over the years. Today it may accompany many dishes, such as seafood, grilled and barbecued meat, and roasts, but remains a vegetarian favorite.

Directions

Trim ends of eggplants and cut into ¼-inch (0.6 cm) thick slices. Place in a small bowl, sprinkle with 1 teaspoon (5 ml) salt, and set aside for 15 minutes. Wash eggplant and wipe dry with paper towels. Add turmeric to eggplant and mix well until slices are coated.

Heat oil in a small skillet or sauté pan over high heat and fry eggplant in batches to a golden brown. Place on paper towels to soak up excess oil.

In another medium sauté pan, heat 1 tablespoon (15 ml) of the used oil over medium heat. Add onions and cook for 3 to 4 minutes until lightly browned. Add green chilies, garlic, spices, and vinegar. Cook for a few seconds, then stir in sugar and coconut milk. Fold in fried eggplant slices and season with salt to taste. Remove from heat. Serve at room temperature.

6 servings

Baba Ghanoush

Baba ghanoush is a rich and flavorful dish. You may use it as a topping for soup or stew or as a small salad.

Directions

Preheat grill. Brush eggplants with 1 tablespoon (15 ml) of the olive oil and place on a hot grill. Turn frequently and grill until skins are blistered and almost burnt and the insides are cooked and soft. Peel and discard skins.

Place eggplants in a colander and let drain. Transfer to a food processor and add the rest of the olive oil, tahini, garlic, shallots, parsley, mint, cumin, lemon juice, and black pepper and season with salt to taste. Pulse a few times to a coarse texture and transfer to a dish. Drizzle with olive oil and sprinkle with the reserved teaspoon of mint.

6 to 8 servings

2 medium round eggplants

¾ cup (180 ml) olive oil, reserve some for drizzling

½ cup (125 ml) tahini

1 tablespoon (15 ml) chopped garlic

3 shallots, chopped fine

¼ cup (60 ml) chopped Italian parsley

¼ cup (60 ml) chopped mint, reserve 1 teaspoon (5 ml)

1 tablespoon (15 ml) ground cumin

Juice of 1 lemon

1 teaspoon (5 ml) ground black pepper

Salt

Hummus

Hummus may be served with toasted bread or chips. For an appealing presentation, pipe it onto cucumber cups, red and green pepper boats, and cherry tomatoes for the hors d'oeuvres tray.

Directions

In a food processor, combine chickpeas, tahini, garlic, cumin, coriander, cayenne pepper, and black pepper and process until smooth. Season mixture with lemon juice and add salt to taste.

Transfer to a bowl and smooth surface with a spoon, leaving a few marks. Drizzle with olive oil.

Yield: 1 pint (500 ml)

1 cup (250 ml) cooked chickpeas

¼ cup (60 ml) tahini

2 teaspoons (10 ml) minced garlic

1 teaspoon (5 ml) ground cumin

1 teaspoon (5 ml) ground coriander

½ teaspoon (2.5 ml) cayenne pepper

½ teaspoon (2.5 ml) black pepper

Juice of 1 lemon

Salt

2 tablespoons (30 ml) olive oil

Orange and Date Relish

1 orange, peeled and cut into segments

¼ cup (60 ml) julienned orange peel

1 cup (250 ml) pitted, diced dates

¼ cup (60 ml) chopped walnuts

½ cup (125 ml) small-diced red onion

¼ cup (60 ml) orange juice

1 tablespoon (15 ml) lemon juice

1 tablespoon (15 ml) balsamic vinegar

2 garlic cloves, grated

1 teaspoon (5 ml) black pepper

Salt

3 to 4 tablespoons (45 to 60 ml) olive oil

1 teaspoon (5 ml) fennel seeds, roasted

½ cup (125 ml) toasted raisin bread croutons

This relish is good over a spinach salad with goat cheese or on a lightly dressed arugula salad. Or toss in a cup of freshly chopped mint leaves and serve with roast lamb.

Directions

In a bowl, combine orange segments and peel, dates, walnuts, and red onion.

For the dressing, whisk together orange and lemon juices, balsamic vinegar, garlic, and black pepper and season with salt to taste. Whisk in olive oil. Pour over fruit mixture, add fennel seeds and croutons, and toss to combine.

6 to 8 servings

Grated Carrot, Orange, and Raisin Relish

1 pound (453 g) peeled carrots

3 tablespoons (45 ml) vegetable oil

½ teaspoon (2.5 ml) cumin seeds

1 teaspoon (5 ml) black mustard seeds

2 green chilies, sliced

6 to 8 curry leaves

2 tablespoons (30 ml) golden raisins

Juice of 1 orange

Lemon juice

Salt

1 teaspoon (5 ml) carom seeds, very lightly roasted and crushed between the fingertips

Serve a small portion of this relish on a salad of arugula dressed with an orange vinaigrette or as an accompaniment to a simple rice and curry meal.

Directions

Coarsely grate carrots and set aside.

In a medium pan, add oil and place over medium heat. When oil is hot, add cumin seeds and mustard seeds and stir. When mustard seeds start to splutter, add green chilies, curry leaves, carrots, raisins, and orange juice. Season with lemon juice and salt to taste. Turn heat to high and cook 30 seconds, stirring constantly. Stir in carom seeds. Transfer to a dish and refrigerate.

8 servings

Mung Bean and Coconut Relish

Occasionally I serve this relish as a salad in lightly dressed butter lettuce cups. If fresh coconut is unavailable, rehydrate dried grated coconut and use as a substitute.

Directions

Clean and wash mung beans in several changes of cold water. Place in a small pan and add water to cover. Bring to a slow simmer over medium heat, using a small ladle to remove and discard the foam that forms on the surface of the water. Simmer for about 20 minutes, until barely cooked through.

Pour into a strainer and drain cooking water, then run cold water over mung beans to cool them down. Make sure beans are completely drained, gently press out any moisture using paper towels, and empty beans into a bowl. Add coconut, cilantro, ginger, green onion, and lemon juice and season with salt to taste. Toss gently.

Heat oil in a small pan over medium heat. Add urad dal and cook a few seconds until the dal turns a light pink. Add red and green chilies, black mustard seeds, and curry leaves. Cook 5 to 6 seconds until mustard seeds splutter. Immediately pour contents of the pan over the seasoned mung beans. Toss lightly.

6 servings

½ cup (125 ml) split mung beans

2 cups (500 ml) water

½ cup (125 ml) grated fresh coconut

¼ cup (60 ml) coarsely chopped cilantro

1 teaspoon (5 ml) chopped ginger

1 tablespoon (15 ml) finely chopped green onion

2 tablespoons (30 ml) lemon juice

Salt

1 tablespoon (15 ml) vegetable oil

1 teaspoon (5 ml) urad dal

2 dried red chilies, broken into pieces and seeded

2 green chilies, sliced thin

½ teaspoon (2.5 ml) black mustard seeds

10 curry leaves

Coconut Relish

This delicious relish is easy to assemble. It is a perfect example of how a few ingredients can add flavor to a meal in a hurry. A spoonful of this relish will spice up leftover grilled meat or chicken. It is also good on cooked chickpeas and diced tomatoes or diced fresh fruit.

Directions

Thoroughly mix all ingredients in a bowl. Add lemon juice and sugar and season with salt to taste. Mix gently to blend flavors.

4 servings

½ cup (125 ml) yogurt, whisked smooth

½ cup (125 ml) grated fresh coconut

2 green chilies, finely chopped

1 shallot, thinly sliced

1 teaspoon (5 ml) black pepper

1 tablespoon (15 ml) lemon juice, or to taste

Sugar

Salt

Mango and Coconut Relish

2 ripe mangoes, peeled

¼ cup (60 ml) grated fresh coconut

1 cup (250 ml) yogurt, whisked until smooth and creamy

1 tablespoon (15 ml) lemon juice

½ teaspoon (2.5 ml) crushed red pepper

½ teaspoon (2.5 ml) black pepper

2 teaspoons (10 ml) sugar, or to taste

Salt

1 tablespoon (15 ml) vegetable oil

1 tablespoon (15 ml) thinly sliced shallots

1 teaspoon (5 ml) julienned ginger

1 green chili, thinly sliced

1 dried red chili, broken into ¼-inch (0.6 cm) pieces and seeded

1 teaspoon (5 ml) black mustard seeds

Select mangoes that are ripe and soft, but not overly ripe. This relish makes a tasty starter and can also be served as a luncheon salad on a hot afternoon.

Directions

Slice mangoes and remove and discard seeds. Cut into ½-inch (1.25 cm) cubes. Place cubed mangoes in a bowl and fold in coconut, yogurt, lemon juice, crushed red pepper, black pepper, and sugar and season with salt to taste. Set aside.

Heat oil in a small sauté pan over medium heat. Add shallots, ginger, and green chili and fry until shallots turn golden. Add red chili and mustard seeds and fry for a few seconds, or until mustard seeds start to splutter. Remove from heat and pour contents over the bowl of seasoned mangoes. Toss to combine. Serve cold.

6 to 8 servings

Cucumbers in Yogurt

2 teaspoons (10 ml) cumin seeds

2 seedless cucumbers, peeled

1 teaspoon (5 ml) salt

1 tablespoon (15 ml) vegetable oil

1 teaspoon (5 ml) black mustard seeds

2 green chilies, chopped

2 shallots, chopped

2 tablespoons (30 ml) chopped cilantro

1 cup (250 ml) yogurt beaten smooth

2 teaspoons (10 ml) black pepper

1 tablespoon (15 ml) lemon juice

This is a lovely salad for a hot afternoon. Yogurt and cucumber both have a cooling quality that makes this salad a perfect accompaniment to a spicy curry. Fage Greek yogurt, a strained yogurt that is thicker than conventional yogurt, works well in this salad.

Directions

Roast cumin seeds in a small sauté pan over low heat until seeds are crisp and brown. Grind coarsely and set aside.

Cut cucumber into very small dice, sprinkle with salt, and place in a strainer. After 10 minutes, squeeze out liquid and transfer cucumbers to a bowl.

Add oil to a small sauté pan over high heat. Add mustard seeds and stir for a few seconds until seeds start to pop. Turn heat to low, add green chilies and shallots, and cook for a few seconds. Remove from heat.

Spoon mixture over diced cucumber and fold in cilantro, yogurt, black pepper, and lemon juice. Toss gently to blend flavors and transfer to a serving dish. Sprinkle with the ground cumin seeds. Serve cold.

8 servings

Cucumber, Onion, and Tomato Relish

This simple relish is a favorite accompaniment to a simple rice and curry meal. It is also good with grilled or sautéed seafood.

Directions

Place ingredients in a dish and add salt to taste. Mix and set aside for 30 minutes before serving.

4 servings

1 cucumber, peeled, seeded, and diced small (about 1 cup [250 ml])

½ cup (125 ml) chopped onion

1 cup (250 ml) small-diced tomato

3 green chilies, seeded and finely chopped

2 tablespoons (30 ml) chopped cilantro

1 teaspoon (5 ml) black pepper

Juice of 1½ lemons

Salt

Bengali Spicy Tomato "Pachadi"

This spicy Bengali preparation is known as a pachadi. The spices used in this recipe are very similar to the spices in Sri Lankan–style cooking. The recipe is easy to make and adds so much taste to a rice and curry meal. It also helps enliven plain fish and chicken dishes.

Directions

In a medium pot, bring water to a boil and carefully drop in tomatoes. Cook 30 seconds, then remove tomatoes and drop into ice water. Allow to cool for 10 minutes before peeling off skins. Place tomatoes on a cutting board and chop fine, almost to a mush.

Heat oil in a medium sauté pan over medium heat. Add onions and curry leaves and cook until the onions are limp. Add cumin seeds and mustard seeds and cook a few seconds, until the mustard seeds start to pop. Stir in cayenne, turmeric, garam masala, and chopped tomatoes. Season with tamarind juice, sugar, and salt to taste. Cook for 5 more minutes and transfer to a dish. Garnish with cilantro sprigs.

Serve at room temperature. Refrigerate leftovers and use within 1 or 2 days.

8 to 10 servings

2 quarts (2 L) water

1 pound (453 g) Roma tomatoes

4 tablespoons (60 ml) vegetable oil

½ cup (125 ml) chopped onions

10 curry leaves

1 teaspoon (5 ml) cumin seeds

1 teaspoon (5 ml) black mustard seeds

1 teaspoon (5 ml) cayenne pepper, or to taste

½ teaspoon (2.5 ml) turmeric

2 teaspoons (10 m) **Garam Masala** (p. 226)

¼ cup (60 ml) tamarind juice

2 teaspoons (10 ml) sugar or to taste

Salt

½ cup (125 ml) broken cilantro sprigs

Charred Tomato Relish

In some parts of Asia, tomatoes and eggplants are baked under hot wood ashes in an open fireplace. The ashes stay hot for a long time in the fireplace after meals have been cooked. These charred grilled tomatoes with a smoky taste are as good as tomatoes baked under hot ashes.

Directions

Heat the grill. Toss tomatoes in oil and place on hot grill. Turn tomatoes and roast until peel is black and blistered.

When cool enough to handle, peel tomatoes and chop into rough-looking chunks. Place in a dish and add shallots, green chilies, crushed red pepper, black pepper, lime juice, sugar (if using), and salt to taste. Mix and then fold in coconut milk. Sprinkle with cumin.

6 servings

3 beefsteak tomatoes

1 tablespoon (15 ml) olive oil

4 shallots, thinly sliced

2 green chilies, thinly sliced

1 teaspoon (5 ml) crushed red pepper

1 teaspoon (5 ml) black pepper

1 tablespoon (15 ml) lime juice

1 teaspoon (5 ml) sugar (optional)

Salt

2 tablespoons (30 ml) thick coconut milk

2 teaspoons (10 ml) cumin seeds, dark-roasted and coarsely ground

Hawaiian Lomilomi Salmon

8 ounces (226 mg) **Salted Salmon** (below)

1 Maui onion, finely chopped

2 medium Kula tomatoes, peeled, seeded, and chopped

1 tablespoon (15 ml) chopped green onion

Crushed ice

Lomilomi salmon is a favorite at luaus and the essential accompaniment to poi. It is also served alone as an appetizer. Salted salmon is the main ingredient, and the excess salt must be removed before making the dish, leaving just enough to balance the flavors of the juicy island tomatoes. Instead of cutting salmon into small dice, you may shred it, which is the traditional way.

Directions

Remove and discard salmon skin and hold salmon under the tap, scrubbing gently with your fingers, and let the running water wash away the excess salt. Remove bones and cut salmon into small dice. Place salmon in a glass or ceramic bowl, then add onion and tomatoes. Mix well and massage seasonings into salmon with your fingers.

Refrigerate for about an hour. Transfer to small individual serving dishes, garnish with green onion, and spoon crushed ice on each portion when ready to serve.

10 to 12 servings

Salted Salmon

2 pounds (907 g) salmon fillet with skin

½ cup (125 ml) sea salt

Cold water

Directions

Coat salmon with salt and place in a nonreactive pan that allows the salmon to stay flat. Cover and refrigerate for 2 days. After 2 days, discard liquid in the pan, barely cover salmon with cold water, and refrigerate for 3 days. After 3 days, remove salmon from water, remove and discard skin, and wash away excess salt. Use to prepare **Lomilomi Salmon** (above).

Yield: 1¾ pounds (793 g)

Hawaiian Fried "Haupia"

Fried haupia is not a relish in the true sense of the word; nevertheless, it is a delicious accompaniment to a rice and curry meal. I use homemade haupia, a favorite Hawaiian preparation, for my fried haupia. Making fresh coconut milk is a tedious process; a good-quality canned coconut milk is an excellent choice for this recipe. Fried haupia is crispy on the outside with a creamy interior. Years ago, I served it as a hot accompaniment to Hawaiian curry and rice, much to the amazement of my guests.

6 tablespoons (90 ml) cornstarch

6 tablespoons (90 ml) sugar

3 cups (750 ml) coconut milk

Salt

1 cup (250 ml) flour

4 eggs, beaten

2 cups (500 ml) panko

Vegetable oil for frying

Directions

In a bowl, combine cornstarch and sugar. Add about a cup or more of coconut milk and stir to make a smooth paste.

In a saucepan, bring remaining coconut milk to a simmer. Gradually stir in cornstarch-and-sugar paste, season with a pinch of salt, and cook over low heat, stirring constantly, until mixture thickens, about 10 minutes. Pour into a square pan to a depth of 1½ inches (3.8 cm) and refrigerate overnight.

The next day, cut haupia into 1-inch (2.5 cm) squares. Take one piece of haupia at a time, coat with flour, dip in beaten eggs, and roll in panko. Cover and refrigerate for at least 2 to 3 hours, so the coating sets firmly.

Heat oil for deep-frying over moderate heat. Fry a few pieces of coated haupia at a time until they turn crispy and golden. Remove and place on paper towels to drain. Serve hot or at room temperature.

8 to 10 servings

Herb Pesto

2 cups (500 ml) mixed herbs (such as mint, parsley, and basil)

2 tablespoons (30 ml) chopped garlic

1 teaspoon (5 ml) salt

¼ cup (60 ml) chopped walnuts

¼ cup (60 ml) grated Parmesan cheese

1 teaspoon (5 ml) black pepper

2 tablespoons (30 ml) water

½ cup (125 ml) olive oil

¼ to ½ cup (60 to 125 ml) Fage Greek yogurt

Pesto is a favorite with vegetarians, especially with pasta. Try it on grilled vegetables and as a salad dressing.

Directions

In a food processor, combine herbs, garlic, salt, walnuts, cheese, black pepper, and water. Process until well blended to a coarse paste. Pour olive oil in gradually and blend. Add yogurt and blend to a coarse, runny paste.

Yield: 1 pint (500 ml)

Pesto

1 cup (250 ml) mixed chopped herbs (such as parsley, basil, and chives)

2 ripe fresh chilies, seeded and chopped

2 slices of white bread, crusts removed

3 anchovy fillets

1 tablespoon (15 ml) sugar

3 tablespoons (45 ml) white wine vinegar

1 teaspoon (5 ml) black pepper

Salt

About ½ cup (125 ml) olive oil

This is an excellent spread for toasted bread and sandwiches and is equally good with cold meat and fish. It comes in handy as a dip for vegetables and crackers and as a sauce for pasta served with a sprinkle of grated pecorino cheese.

Directions

Place ingredients in a blender and blend, gradually drizzling in the olive oil, until mixture has a smooth texture. Transfer to a container and store in the refrigerator. Use within a day or two.

Yield: 1½ cups (375 ml)

Minty Cashew Pesto

This is one of my favorite dips for toasted pita bread chips. It is also a tasty spread; use with sliced tomatoes for a delicious sandwich. Try pasta with tomato sauce and this pesto, a favorite dish of vegetarians.

Directions

In a food processor, combine herbs, cashews, and garlic and process to a coarse texture. Add olive oil in a stream while the processor is running. Season pesto with black pepper and lemon juice and add salt to taste. Add sour cream and blend. If pesto is too stiff, add a tablespoon of hot water and blend. Transfer to a container, cover, and refrigerate until ready to use. Keeps for a day or two.

Yield: 1½ cups (375 ml)

1 cup (250 ml) mint leaves

1 cup (250 ml) chopped parsley

½ cup (125 ml) raw cashew nuts

4 garlic cloves, minced

½ cup (125 ml) olive oil

1 teaspoon (5 ml) black pepper

2 tablespoons (30 ml) lemon juice

Salt

½ cup (125 ml) sour cream or yogurt

Hot water

Mint and Coconut Relish

This relish is commonly served with Indian savory pastries, breads, and rice dishes. Try it with your favorite lamb dish.

Directions

In a food processor, grind coconut, mint, yogurt, chilies, onion, ginger, sugar, and lemon juice to a smooth paste. Season with salt to taste and serve in a mound in a small dish.

6 servings

1 cup (250 ml) grated fresh coconut

1½ cups (375 ml) fresh mint leaves

¼ cup (60 ml) yogurt

2 green chilies, chopped

1 tablespoon (15 ml) chopped onion

1 tablespoon (15 ml) chopped ginger

2 teaspoons (10 ml) sugar, or to taste

2 tablespoons (30 ml) lemon or lime juice

Salt

Roasted Garlic with Honey and Balsamic Vinegar

3 tablespoons (45 ml) olive oil

1 tablespoon (15 ml) balsamic vinegar

¼ teaspoon (1.25 ml) cayenne pepper

¼ teaspoon (1.25 ml) black pepper

1 teaspoon (5 ml) lemon juice

½ cup (125 ml) salt

4 whole heads of garlic

¼ cup (60 ml) honey

There are many varieties of garlic. For this recipe, use large, whole heads of garlic, preferably the light purplish variety that is plump and fleshy. Roasted garlic is always good partnered with crusty hot bread and dips.

Directions

For the balsamic dip, whisk 2 tablespoons of the olive oil, balsamic vinegar, cayenne, black pepper, and lemon juice in a small bowl. Set aside.

Preheat oven to 300°F (150°C). Place salt in a small skillet and smooth out to form an even layer. Cut the tops off the garlic, brush the cut sides with the remaining tablespoon of olive oil, and place the garlic on the salt, cut side up.

Cover the skillet with a lid and place in the oven. Roast garlic for 30 minutes, then remove the lid and brush the cut tops with honey. Replace the lid and roast 10 minutes or until the garlic is cooked and soft.

When done, take out of the oven, remove the lid, and brush garlic tops again with honey, reserving the extra honey for the dip. Arrange roasted garlic on a serving dish. Serve with hot bread, the balsamic dip, and honey.

6 to 8 servings

Spiced Dal "On the Side"

Dal is a favorite accompaniment to Indian and Sri Lankan main dishes. Just a bowl of this spicy dal can make a meal complete. The spicing is unique and adds fragrance to the dish, while heat from the chilies will awaken sluggish appetites.

Directions

Wash dal in several changes of water and place in a medium heavy-bottomed pan. Add water, turmeric, ground coriander, and ginger and bring to a simmer, uncovered, over medium heat. Remove and discard the froth that forms on the surface of the water. Cook for 15 to 20 minutes, or until dal is soft. Stir in tamarind and season with salt to taste. Set aside.

In a small sauté pan, heat oil over medium heat. When oil is hot, add mustard seeds and cumin seeds. Using a wooden spoon, stir until the seeds start to pop (this takes only a few seconds). Immediately add shallots, chilies, curry leaves, and garlic and stir until shallots turn a deep golden color.

Pour contents of the sauté pan over the cooked dal. Stir in coconut milk and simmer for 2 minutes. Spoon into a deep medium bowl. Serve with rice or Indian breads.

6 to 8 servings

1½ cups (375 ml) masoor dal

4 cups (1 L) water

¼ teaspoon (1.25 ml) turmeric

1 teaspoon (5 ml) ground coriander

1 tablespoon (15 ml) finely chopped ginger

1 tablespoon (15 ml) tamarind pulp

Salt

2 tablespoons (30 ml) vegetable oil

½ teaspoon (2.5 ml) black mustard seeds

½ teaspoon (2.5 ml) cumin seeds

2 tablespoons (30 ml) sliced shallots

3 whole dried red chilies, broken into 3 pieces each and seeded

10 curry leaves

1 teaspoon (5 ml) chopped garlic

½ cup (125 ml) thick coconut milk

Tomato Relish for Fried Okra

1 medium red onion

4 plum tomatoes, diced small

1 green chili, seeded and thinly sliced

1 teaspoon (5 ml) black pepper

1 tablespoon (15 ml) lime juice

1 tablespoon (15 ml) apple cider vinegar

1 tablespoon (15 ml) coarsely chopped cilantro

Salt

This simple tomato relish gets its tartness from lots of lemon juice, and the green chili and black pepper provide the right amount of heat. Its bright flavors go well with crisp deep-fried food.

Directions

Cut onions into small dice. Place in a strainer and rinse with cold water to wash away the strong taste and smell. Drain well.

Transfer onions to a bowl, add the remaining ingredients, and season with salt to taste. Mix well. Serve as a dip in a small bowl.

6 to 8 servings

Eggplant Raita

1 round eggplant, about 8 ounces (226 g)

2 tablespoons (30 ml) vegetable oil

1½ cups (375 ml) yogurt

1 teaspoon (5 ml) crushed red pepper

1 teaspoon (5 ml) black pepper

¼ cup (60 ml) chopped mint

¼ cup (60 ml) sliced green onions

¼ cup (60 ml) thinly sliced red onion

1 teaspoon (5 ml) cumin seeds

1 tablespoon (15 ml) lemon juice

Salt

Eggplant raita is a favorite accompaniment to Indian breads and rich, spicy rice dishes. This would also be a refreshing side dish with poultry, lamb, and other meat dishes.

Directions

Heat grill. Rub eggplant with about 1 tablespoon (15 ml) of the oil and place on the grill. Cook, turning frequently, until the skin is scorched, blistered, and smoking and the inside is cooked and soft. Remove from the grill and set aside. When cool enough to handle, peel eggplant and chop into bite-size pieces.

Place yogurt in a medium bowl and whisk until yogurt is smooth. Add crushed red pepper, black pepper, mint, and green onions. Add chopped eggplant to seasoned yogurt and mix to combine with seasonings.

Heat reserved tablespoon of oil in a small sauté pan over medium heat. Add red onion slices and cook until wilted. Add cumin seeds and cook until seeds start to splutter. Immediately pour the contents of the pan over the yogurt-eggplant mixture. Season with lemon juice, salt to taste, and fold into the eggplant-yogurt mixture. Spoon into a medium serving dish and serve.

6 to 8 servings

Potatoes with Cucumber and Yogurt Dressing

This is a spicy yet refreshing accompaniment to hot barbecued meat and Indian breads. It is also a fresh, healthful alternative to mayonnaise-laden potato salad.

Directions

Grate cucumber, sprinkle with 1 teaspoon (5 ml) salt, and place in a strainer. Let sit for 10 minutes, then press out liquid from cucumber and place in a bowl.

Cut potatoes into ½-inch (1.25 cm) cubes and place in a bowl. Add green onions, crushed red pepper, ground cumin seeds, and black pepper and season with salt to taste. Toss to combine seasonings with potatoes.

Add yogurt to the cucumber and whisk together. Pour over the potatoes and toss to combine. Transfer to a fresh dish and sprinkle with garam masala and dill.

6 servings

1 seedless cucumber, peeled

Salt

½ pound (226 g) potatoes, peeled and boiled

½ cup (125 ml) sliced green onions

1 teaspoon (5 ml) crushed red pepper

1 teaspoon (5 ml) roasted, coarsely ground cumin seeds

2 teaspoons (10 ml) black pepper

2 cups (500 ml) yogurt

2 teaspoons (10 ml) **Garam Masala** (p. 226)

½ cup (125 ml) snipped dill

Cucumber Relish with Coconut Milk Dressing

1 cucumber, peeled and thinly sliced

1 teaspoon (5 ml) salt

1 jalapeño, seeded and thinly sliced

1 tablespoon (15 ml) thinly sliced shallots

½ teaspoon (2.5 ml) black pepper

1 tablespoon (15 ml) lime juice

2 tablespoons (30 ml) thick coconut milk

This dish is a Sri Lankan favorite with rice and curry. I also offer it alongside barbecued or spicy grilled meat. The relish should be mixed just before serving.

Directions

Mix cucumber with salt and set aside for 10 minutes. Place in a strainer, press out liquid, and transfer cucumber to a bowl. Refrigerate until ready to assemble the relish.

When ready to serve the relish, add jalapeño, shallots, black pepper, and lime juice to the cucumber. Mix thoroughly and fold in coconut milk. Serve cold.

6 servings

Pomelo Relish

Pomelo is a lovely fruit. On average, it is as large as a football. The skin and pith are so thick that it takes skill to get to the edible part of the fruit. A sharp knife is essential.

Children and grown-ups love to dip the prepared fruit into a fast-pickling mix and make a feast of it. As children, our favorite was coconut vinegar seasoned with prepared mustard, crushed red pepper, crushed jaggery, ground cinnamon, black pepper, and salt. We also use pomelo in a salad dressed in a sweet-and-sour vinaigrette. This Hawaiian pomelo relish is a fancy accompaniment to grilled seafood.

Directions

With a sharp knife, peel pomelo and remove the pith along with the skin. Cut the fruit into segments, then remove and discard any pith and bitter membranes attached to the segments. Break segments into 1-inch (2.5 cm) pieces and place in a dish.

In a bowl, whisk together vinegar, lemon juice, crushed red pepper, mustard, and brown sugar or jaggery. Pour over fruit. Cover and let marinate for 1 to 2 hours.

Add grated apple, ginger, and green onions to the marinated fruit and toss to combine. Add romaine lettuce, shallots, and mint leaves and season with sea salt to taste. Toss to combine. Transfer to a dish and sprinkle with cashews, cumin, and black and white sesame seeds. Add more sea salt if needed and serve.

6 to 8 servings

2 cups (500 ml) peeled and segmented pomelo

2 tablespoons (30 ml) white wine vinegar

2 tablespoons (30 ml) lemon juice

2 teaspoons (10 ml) crushed red pepper

1 tablespoon (15 ml) Dijon mustard

2 tablespoons (30 ml) brown sugar or crushed jaggery to taste

1 green apple, peeled, cored, and coarsely grated

1 tablespoon (15 ml) coarsely grated ginger

1 tablespoon (15 ml) sliced green onion

1 cup (250 ml) sliced romaine lettuce

2 tablespoons (30 ml) sliced shallots

½ cup (125 ml) mint leaves

Sea salt

½ cup (125 ml) chopped roasted cashew nuts

1 teaspoon (5 ml) crushed dark-roasted cumin seeds

½ teaspoon (2.5 ml) roasted black sesame seeds

½ teaspoon (2.5 ml) roasted white sesame seeds

Ogo Relish

1 cup (250 ml) ogo

3 plum tomatoes, diced small

1 tablespoon (15 ml) chopped red onion

1 tablespoon (15 ml) chopped green onion

1 tablespoon (15 ml) chopped mint

2 tablespoons (30 ml) rice wine vinegar

1 tablespoon (15 ml) fish sauce

1 tablespoon (15 ml) soy sauce

1 tablespoon (15 ml) crushed red pepper

1 tablespoon (15 ml) mirin

Lemon juice

Salt

Ogo is a type of seaweed and a favorite in Hawai'i. This relish is perfect on seafood kebabs.

Directions

Trim off the tough ends of the ogo and wash well. Cut into ½-inch (1.25 cm) lengths and place in a small bowl.

In another small bowl, mix remaining ingredients and season with salt to taste. Pour over ogo, toss, and serve in a glass dish.

6 servings

Orange, Fennel, and Red Onion Relish

4 oranges

1 fennel bulb, with a few fronds reserved

1 red onion, thinly sliced

1 teaspoon (5 ml) crushed red pepper

1 teaspoon (5 ml) cracked black pepper

Juice of 1 lemon

Salt

Fennel has a refreshing taste, and this relish, with its citrusy seasoning, is a lovely accompaniment to seafood.

Directions

Peel oranges and remove pith, then separate segments and remove membranes. Thinly shave fennel bulb. Wash the reserved fronds, wrap in paper towels, and refrigerate.

Place orange segments, shaved fennel, onion, crushed red pepper, black pepper, and lemon juice in a medium bowl, add salt to taste, and toss lightly. Marinate 1 hour. Transfer to a medium dish and garnish with fennel fronds.

6 to 8 servings

Brandade

Brandade, a dish from Provence, France, is a delicious puree of salt cod. I learned to cook with cod while apprenticing in France. Brandade makes a perfect accompaniment to breakfast omelets or poached eggs and toast. Salt cod, the main ingredient, must be purged of almost all its salt. Be careful not to overcook, or the fish will be tough.

Directions

Place salt cod in a medium nonreactive container, such as a stainless steel half-size hotel pan. Add enough cold water to cover the cod. Refrigerate, uncovered, for 48 hours, changing water 4 to 5 times and covering with cold water each time. Drain cod, place in a medium saucepot, and add enough cold water to cover. Cook over low heat for 20 minutes until the flesh is tender. Remove cod from poaching liquid. Check for and remove any remaining bones and skin.

While the cod is still warm, place it in a food processor with the garlic and process until fluffy. Gradually add potatoes in very small quantities and process until ingredients are well combined. Drizzle olive oil and then hot cream into the mixture, process, and season with pepper. Taste and add a pinch of salt only if needed. Fold in parsley.

Transfer to a shallow, oven-safe dish, dust with grated Parmesan cheese, and broil for 1 to 2 minutes.

6 to 8 servings

¾ pound (340 g) salt cod, skinned and boned

1 tablespoon (15 ml) pureed roasted garlic

¼ pound (113 g) potatoes, peeled, boiled, and crushed (about ½ cup)

About 3 ounces (88 ml) olive oil

¾ cup (180 ml) hot cream

1 teaspoon (5 ml) black pepper

1 tablespoon (15 ml) chopped parsley

1 tablespoon (15 ml) grated Parmesan cheese

Blood Orange and Mint Relish

4 blood oranges, peeled and cut into segments

¼ cup (60 ml) mint leaves, thickly sliced

1 tablespoon (15 ml) lemon juice

1 teaspoon (5 ml) chopped chives

1 tablespoon (15 ml) honey

¼ cup (60 ml) olive oil

Black pepper

Sea salt

¼ cup (60 ml) dried coconut chips

½ teaspoon (2.5 ml) toasted black sesame seeds

1 tablespoon (15 ml) onion flakes

In small portions, this relish makes a delicious starter. I also serve it with grilled fish.

Directions

Place blood orange segments and mint in a medium glass dish.

In a small bowl, whisk together lemon juice, chives, honey, and olive oil and season with black pepper and sea salt to taste. Pour over blood oranges and toss to combine. Refrigerate and let marinate for 10 to 15 minutes.

Spoon into a small, flat serving dish. Sprinkle coconut chips, sesame seeds, and onion flakes on top and serve.

6 to 8 servings

Sicilian Hot Relish

The salty anchovy is the key ingredient that makes this hot relish so special. The touch of sweetness from the tomatoes counteracts the heat of the chilies and balances the saltiness of the anchovies. The relish is excellent with seafood.

Directions

Heat olive oil in a small sauté pan over low heat. Add onion and cook until soft. Add garlic, chilies, cayenne pepper, and anchovies and cook for a few minutes. Add tomatoes, olives, and capers, season with salt to taste, and cook for about 15 minutes. Fold in lemon zest. The relish should be moist, not runny or dry. Serve warm.

Yield: 2 cups (500 ml)

2 tablespoons (30 ml) olive oil

1 small onion, chopped fine

1 tablespoon (15 ml) minced garlic

1 tablespoon (15 ml) finely chopped hot chilies

½ teaspoon (2.5 ml) cayenne pepper

1 tablespoon (15 ml) finely chopped anchovies

1 cup (250 ml) Roma tomatoes, seeded and chopped fine

¼ cup (60 ml) chopped green olives

1 tablespoon (15 ml) **capers**, chopped coarse

Salt

Zest of 1 lemon

Harissa

Harissa is a spicy condiment. It is easy to make and adds fiery flavor to bland food.

Directions

Soak chilies in water for at least 30 minutes. Strain and discard soaking water.

Heat a small skillet over medium heat and roast coriander and cumin seeds until seeds are crisp. In a spice grinder, grind them to a fine powder.

Using a mortar and pestle, crush and grind garlic, soaked chilies, and ground coriander and cumin seeds with salt to taste until the mixture is a smooth paste. (You may use a hand blender instead.) Pour olive oil into the mixture in a stream and continue to grind with a rolling motion until the mixture is emulsified. Transfer to a jar, cover tightly, and refrigerate. The harissa keeps well for 2 to 3 weeks.

Yield: 1 cup (250 ml)

24 dried hot red chilies, stems removed

About ¾ cup (180 ml) water

1 tablespoon (15 ml) coriander seeds

1 tablespoon (15 ml) cumin seeds

4 garlic cloves, roughly chopped

1 teaspoon (5 ml) salt

¼ cup (60 ml) olive oil

Tapenade

½ pound (226 g) Niçoise olives

½ pound (226 g) pitted black Greek olives

1 tablespoon (15 ml) capers, drained

4 anchovy fillets, dried

2 garlic cloves, minced

½ teaspoon (2.5 ml) chopped thyme leaves

1 teaspoon (5 ml) Dijon mustard

Freshly ground black pepper

Lemon juice

2 tablespoons (30 ml) olive oil

Salt

Tapenade is a popular preparation in France. Its seasonings are associated with the Provence region. The flavorful spread is delicious on crostini and crackers or tossed with hot pasta.

Directions

In a food processor, combine olives, capers, anchovies, garlic, thyme, and mustard with black pepper to taste. Blend, gradually adding lemon juice and olive oil, until the mixture has a coarse texture, with tiny bits of olives still visible. Taste and add salt if needed. Refrigerate.

Yield: 2 cups (500 ml)

Tomato Relish with Goat Cheese

1 pound (453 g) heirloom tomatoes

¼ cup (60 ml) finely chopped red onion

¼ cup (60 ml) julienned lemon zest

1 teaspoon (5 ml) roasted cumin seeds

1 teaspoon (5 ml) coarsely crushed black pepper

¼ cup (60 ml) lemon juice

1 tablespoon (15 ml) balsamic vinegar

2 teaspoons (10 ml) sugar

2 tablespoons (30 ml) olive oil

Salt

½ cup (125 ml) goat cheese

2 teaspoons (10 ml) garlic flakes

2 teaspoons (10 ml) chopped thyme leaves

Served in small portions with crostini, this relish makes a great starter. Or dress it up with crisp greens for a salad. I use heirloom tomatoes or Kula tomatoes, but other ripe tomatoes will work as well.

Directions

Cut tomatoes into wedges and place in a bowl. Add onion and lemon zest. Toss to combine. Add cumin seeds, black pepper, lemon juice, balsamic vinegar, sugar, and olive oil with salt to taste. Toss to coat tomatoes with seasonings and marinate for 30 minutes.

Spoon into small individual relish dishes. Crumble goat cheese over, sprinkle with garlic flakes and thyme, and serve.

6 to 8 servings

Chermoula

This is an interesting relish that can be spooned over stews and soups or served as a dip for fried fish. It can also be used as a marinade for fish that will be dipped in flour and deep-fried or grilled.

Directions

Place olive oil, vinegar, lemon, cumin, cayenne pepper, and paprika in a food processor and blend a few seconds. Add red chilies, cilantro, mint, and garlic with salt to taste. Pulse a few seconds to combine until mixture has a rough consistency. Use fresh.

Yield: 1 cup (250 ml)

¼ cup (60 ml) olive oil

2 tablespoons (30 ml) distilled vinegar

Juice of 1 lemon

1 teaspoon (5 ml) ground cumin

1 teaspoon (5 ml) cayenne pepper

1 teaspoon (5 ml) paprika

4 fresh hot red chilies, seeded and chopped fine

½ cup (125 ml) cilantro

½ cup (125 ml) mint leaves

1 tablespoon (15 ml) minced garlic

Salt

Fresh Coriander Relish

Fresh coriander leaves with tender stems, or a combination of coriander, mint, and parsley, may be used in this recipe. This is a common relish served with chapati, dosa, or rice. Try it with grilled seafood. Not everybody likes asafetida, so you may omit it if you prefer.

Directions

Place grated coconut and chopped cilantro leaves in a bowl.

Heat oil in a small sauté pan over medium heat, add urad dal and chilies, and fry for 1 or 2 minutes until the chilies are wilted. Add asafetida (if using), immediately remove from heat, and add contents of pan to the coconut and cilantro. Add tamarind, jaggery, and lime juice and salt to taste.

In a blender, grind all to a smooth paste. Mound relish in a small serving dish and serve at room temperature.

Yield: 1½ cups (375 ml)

½ cup (125 ml) unsweetened grated fresh coconut

2 packed cups (500 ml) chopped coriander leaves with tender stems

1 tablespoon (15 ml) vegetable oil

2 tablespoons (30 ml) urad dal

2 green chilies, stems removed

Large pinch of asafetida (optional)

2 tablespoons (30 ml) tamarind juice

1 tablespoon (15 ml) jaggery or dark brown sugar

Lime or lemon juice

Salt

Rouille

1 thick slice white bread, crusts removed

1 tablespoon (15 ml) heavy cream or milk

4 egg yolks

1 tablespoon (15 ml) minced garlic

1 tablespoon (15 ml) hot water

About 6 ounces (177 ml) olive oil

½ teaspoon (2.5 ml) black pepper

¼ teaspoon (1.25 ml) cayenne pepper

1 tablespoon (15 ml) lemon juice

Salt

Rouille is a garlicky, spicy-hot sauce thickened with cream-soaked bread and egg yolks and emulsified with olive oil. This French preparation is very much like mayonnaise except for the pasty texture that results from the addition of bread. I like to enliven the rouille with a squeeze of lemon juice. Serve with grilled seafood, spoon on soups or stews, or serve with steamed vegetables. Any leftover rouille should be discarded.

Directions

In a bowl, soak bread in cream.

Combine egg yolks, minced garlic, and hot water in a food processor and blend a few seconds. Squeeze bread to remove most of the cream and add bread to egg yolks. Blend a few seconds to incorporate the bread. Continue to blend while adding olive oil in a steady stream. Add black pepper, cayenne pepper, lemon juice, and salt to taste and continue to blend a few seconds more until rouille is soft and fluffy. Serve in a small bowl with a small spoon.

Yield: 1½ cups (375 ml)

Charred Butternut Squash and Tomato Relish

Char vegetables on a hot grill or in a very hot skillet. The charred vegetables take well to the sweet, sour, mustardy hot dressing. A small serving of this salad with a piece of grilled fish are a satisfying meal for me.

Directions

Preheat a large, wide iron skillet.

Slice butternut squash into ½-inch (1.25 cm) diagonal slices. Place in a container along with onions and tomatoes. Add 2 to 3 teaspoons (10 to 15 ml) of the olive oil, reserving the rest for the dressing, and mix to coat. Char the vegetables in the hot skillet. Remove vegetables and set aside. Turn off heat but keep the skillet on the burner.

Add garlic to the skillet, stirring to prevent burning, until garlic is cooked through. Place the charred vegetables and cooked garlic in a bowl and add parsley, ground chilies, walnuts, and black pepper.

In a small bowl, whisk vinegars, maple syrup, mustard, lemon and orange juices, and orange zest. Whisk in the remaining olive oil and season with salt to taste. Pour just enough dressing over vegetables and toss. Sprinkle a pinch of sea salt on the salad.

8 to 10 servings

1 small butternut squash, peeled, quartered, and seeded

1 onion, cut into 1-inch (2.5 cm) pieces

1 cup (250 ml) grape tomatoes, halved lengthwise

10 garlic cloves, partially crushed

½ cup (125 ml) olive oil

½ cup (125 ml) Italian parsley leaves

6 dried red chilies, roasted and ground to a coarse texture

½ cup (125 ml) walnuts, roasted

2 teaspoons (10 ml) black pepper

2 tablespoons (10 ml) balsamic vinegar

1 tablespoon (15 ml) apple cider vinegar

1 tablespoon (15 ml) maple syrup

1 tablespoon (15 ml) Dijon grainy mustard

1 tablespoon (15 ml) lemon juice

¼ cup (60 ml) orange juice

1 tablespoon (15 ml) grated orange zest

Sea salt

Dill Raita

1 cup (250 ml) Fage Greek yogurt

½ cup (125 ml) finely chopped fresh dill, reserve 1 tablespoon for garnish

1 teaspoon (5 ml) chopped ginger

½ teaspoon (2.5 ml) ground black pepper

Lemon juice

Salt

1 tablespoon (15 ml) olive oil

2 teaspoons (10 ml) sliced shallots

½ teaspoon (2.5 ml) dill seeds, slightly crushed

This raita is laden with dill and is a delicious dip to serve with a roasted vegetable platter. It is good with curries, especially seafood curries, and as a dressing for salads. For a fast salad, toss cubed tomatoes, sliced onions, and green chilies with dill raita.

Directions

In a medium bowl, lightly beat yogurt, then whisk in dill, ginger, and black pepper. Add lemon juice and salt to taste and whisk to combine well.

Heat olive oil in a small sauté pan over medium heat. Add sliced shallots and cook to a dark golden color. Stir in dill seeds and cook for a few seconds, then remove from heat. Fold the contents of the pan into the yogurt mixture to combine. Spoon raita into a medium serving dish, sprinkle with the reserved chopped dill, and serve.

4 to 5 servings

Spinach Raita

Freshly cooked spinach cloaked in tart, spicy yogurt is delicious and cooling when served with tandoori dishes or hot curries. By itself, it is an appetizing dish that vegetarians love. The final touch is the addition of fried spices that give fragrance.

Directions

Whisk yogurt in a bowl and refrigerate.

Place spinach in a large sauté pan, add water, and cook over high heat. With a pair of tongs, move spinach around in the hot pan until wilted, about 1 or 2 minutes. Remove spinach, leaving any liquid that remains in the hot pan. Place spinach in a strainer and press out excess liquid with a spoon. Let cool, chop coarsely, and add to yogurt. Fold in crushed red pepper and black pepper and add salt to taste.

Heat vegetable oil in a small sauté pan over high heat. Add cumin seeds, fenugreek seeds, and mustard seeds and fry until seeds start to pop. Immediately pour spices over the yogurt-spinach mixture and fold to combine flavors. Spoon into a medium serving dish.

6 to 8 servings

1½ cups (375 ml) Fage Greek yogurt

5 cups (1250 ml) spinach leaves, washed and trimmed

1 tablespoon (15 ml) water

¼ teaspoon (1.25 ml) crushed red pepper

¼ teaspoon (1.25 ml) black pepper

Salt

1 tablespoon (15 ml) vegetable oil

1 teaspoon (5 ml) cumin seeds

¼ teaspoon (1.25 ml) fenugreek seeds

½ teaspoon (2.5 ml) black mustard seeds

Spiced Yogurt

1 cup (250 ml) Fage Greek yogurt

1 large shallot, peeled

2 green chilies, sliced

1-inch (2.5 cm) piece of ginger, sliced

½ cup (125 ml) fresh grated coconut

1 tablespoon (15 ml) lime juice

Salt

1 tablespoon (15 ml) vegetable oil

1 tablespoon (15 ml) chana dal

½ teaspoon (2.5 ml) cumin seeds

1 teaspoon (5 ml) black mustard seeds

6 to 8 curry leaves

2 dried red chilies, each broken into
two pieces and seeded

⅛ teaspoon (0.6 ml) asafetida

This spiced yogurt is hot, creamy, sweet, and sour. It is rich with spices, yet its refreshing and cooling qualities make it an elegant addition to a hot summer meal. Spoon it on salad greens, fruit, and vegetables, or serve it with grilled fish or grilled or roasted vegetables. Needless to say, it is a perfect accompaniment to a rice and curry meal.

Directions

Spoon yogurt into a small bowl and set aside. In a blender, grind shallots, green chilies, ginger, and coconut into a paste and whisk into yogurt. Add lime juice and season with salt to taste.

Heat oil in a small pan over medium heat. Add chana dal and fry until it turns a light gold color. Add cumin seeds, mustard seeds, curry leaves, and chilies and fry until mustard seeds start to pop (this takes only a few seconds). Add asafetida and immediately remove from heat.

Spoon the contents of the pan into the yogurt and fold to combine flavors. Let cool.

6 servings

SPICED STUFFED PICKLED LEMONS	MAUI ONION PICKLES
SPICY PICKLED LEMON SLICES	ONION AND CHILI PICKLES
HOT AND SPICY LIME PICKLES	PICKLED RED ONION RINGS
SALTED LEMON WEDGES	PICKLED WHOLE ONIONS
PICKLED GRAPE TOMATOES	BITTER MELON PICKLES
PICKLED BEETS	PICKLED OKRA
PICKLED CHERRIES	PICKLED STUFFED DATES
PICKLED GRAPES	PICKLED PAPAYAS
"SINHALA ACHAHARU"	WHITE ASPARAGUS VINAIGRETTE
CUCUMBER PICKLES	EGGPLANT "PAHI"
SPICY PICKLES	PINEAPPLE PICKLES
JAGGERY PICKLES WITH FRUIT AND DATES	HANDY SWEET PICKLING SYRUP
FAST PICKLED FRUIT	SWEET CARROT PICKLES
FAST MUSTARD PICKLES	PICKLED RADISHES
SWEET CITRUS PICKLES	PICKLED KUMQUATS
STUFFED PICKLED WAX PEPPERS	PICKLED PUMPKIN
PICKLED CAULIFLOWER	SWEET AND SOUR PICKLED PEARS
RIPE MANGO PICKLES	CINNAMON-Y APPLE PICKLES
INDIAN GREEN MANGO PICKLES	WI APPLE PICKLES
GREEN MANGO PICKLES	PICKLED WATERMELON RIND
	PICKLED PLUMS

PICKLES

Pickling is the process of flavoring and preserving fruit, vegetables, eggs, meat, and seafood in seasoned brine. Vinegar is the main ingredient used for pickling. The simplest form of pickling is to brine the food first and then cover it with hot or cold vinegar. Seasonings such as herbs, spices, lemon or lime juice, salt, and sugar add more flavor and reduce the tartness of vinegar. Similar to vinegar, alcohol, such as brandy and wine, used for pickling is both a flavoring and a preservative.

Ingredients that add texture, fragrance, and complex flavors to pickles include spices such as black pepper, fenugreek, nutmeg, cloves, and cinnamon; yellow, white, or black mustard seeds; seasonings such as fresh grated or slivered horseradish root, hot green chilies and dried red chilies, ginger, garlic, and Dijon grainy or ground mustard. Vinegar combined with ground mustard makes a thick, deeply flavored sauce for certain pickles.

The ancient art of pickling is still practiced in Indian households. In India and Sri Lanka, pickles are known as "jewels" of the larder. In India, people frequently use vegetable oils, especially mustard oil, sesame oil, and peanut oil, in pickles. These oil-based Indian pickles most often are strong in taste, pungent, and somewhat salty. They need to marinate for three to six weeks before they are ready to be served.

Some pickles are sun-dried after brining. In India, most pickles are preserved by exposure to the strong summer sunlight. Intense hot sunlight acts as an antiseptic, kills bacteria, and helps prevent fermentation, mold, and mildew. Lime and lemon pickles made by this process will last ten to twelve years. Like wine, they mature with time. Some uncooked pickles that are coated in a spicy brine solution and left for one to three months to mature can also last as long as ten to twelve years. Pickles improve with age. My mother always had a few jars of gorgeous sun-dried lime pickles on hand. Such pickles are culinary treasures. They are piquant and pleasing and add zest to the dishes they accompany. They are palate teasers, stimulate appetites, aid digestion, and enrich menus.

This chapter contains recipes for a variety of pickles. Some can be served soon after preparation and are known for their simplicity and unique flavor. Pickles range from sweet to sour, from mild to fiery hot, from subtle to spine-tingling. It is always best to buy fruits and vegetables from open markets or produce stands. Waxed fruits and vegetables are not suitable for pickling, as the wax prevents them from absorbing vinegar. All fruits and vegetables should be trimmed, washed, and completely dry before use.

For pickling, use only nonreactive utensils and equipment. Store pickles in sterilized glass jars, seal, and place in a cool, dry place. Once a jar is opened, cover it tightly and refrigerate.

Spiced Stuffed Pickled Lemons

Spicy pickled lemon wedges go well with roasted or braised lamb and are especially good with rice and curry meals.

Directions

Wash and dry 6 of the lemons. Make 4 cuts lengthwise on each lemon, leaving wedges attached at stem end.

In a small bowl, mix together salt, cumin seeds, black pepper, and crushed red pepper. Gently stuff lemons with mixture, pressing wedges back together. Place stuffed lemons in a sterilized jar and push them down so they are tightly packed. Sprinkle leftover salt-and-spices mixture onto lemons, then drop in cinnamon stick and red chilies.

Cover jar with a piece of cheesecloth and secure tightly with a rubber band or by tying the cheesecloth in place with cord. Leave in a warm place, preferably in the hot sun, for 3 days and move to the refrigerator by evening.

On the third day, remove and discard cheesecloth. With a sterilized spoon, press gently on lemons and pour the juices in the jar into a small nonreactive pan. Wash and dry remaining 6 lemons, juice the lemons, and add juice to the pan. Bring combined juices to a boil and pour over stuffed lemons. Cover jar with a fresh piece of cheesecloth and secure tightly. Set the jar in a warm place, preferably in the hot sun, during the day and move to the refrigerator by evening. Continue for 3 days, shaking jar once a day.

On the third day, discard cheesecloth and cover the jar with a sterilized lid. Refrigerate. Let sit for a month before serving.

Yield: 1 pint (500 ml)

12 large lemons

4 tablespoons (60 ml) kosher salt

2 tablespoons (30 ml) crushed cumin seeds

1 teaspoon (5 ml) cracked black pepper

½ teaspoon (2.5 ml) crushed red pepper

4-inch (10 cm) piece of cinnamon stick

6 whole red chilies

Spicy Pickled Lemon Slices

6 large lemons

3 tablespoons (15 ml) sea salt

6 whole dried red chilies, stems removed

1 teaspoon (5 ml) whole coriander seeds

1 teaspoon (5 ml) cumin seeds

1 tablespoon (15 ml) black mustard seeds

½ teaspoon (2.5 ml) asafetida

½ teaspoon (2.5 ml) turmeric

2 tablespoons (30 ml) vegetable oil

Pickles are a standby for vegetarians. Although I was not brought up as a vegetarian, I always loved pickles. When we were children, pickles held an important place in our lives as a substitute for candy, because children did not eat much candy.

Pickles may be used in food in numerous ways. Chopped citrus pickles may be used in dressings, sauces, and glazes, especially for roasts and barbecues. A few slices of pickled lemon added when roasting fish will transform the look and taste of the dish. Pickling is not as complicated as it sounds. The recipe given here is easy to make.

Directions

Cut lemons crosswise into ¼-inch (0.6 cm) slices. Place in a bowl, add salt, and mix until lemon slices are coated.

Place red chilies and coriander seeds in a small skillet over medium-low heat and stir with a wooden spoon. Roast until chilies start to brown and coriander seeds are crispy, about 4 to 5 minutes. Add cumin seeds and black mustard seeds and roast 1 to 2 minutes. Turn off heat and add asafetida and turmeric. Cool and grind to a coarse texture in a spice grinder or blender.

Heat oil in a medium nonreactive pan over high heat. Add ground spices and stir for 2 seconds. Remove pan from heat, fold in lemon slices, and set aside to cool.

Transfer to a sterilized jar, cover, and leave overnight. The next day, refrigerate and store for 2 weeks before serving.

Yield: 1 pint (500 ml)

Hot and Spicy Lime Pickles

Lime pickles are a great staple for the pantry. They partner well with seafood dishes and are a good substitute for pickled lemons.

Directions

Slice limes crosswise about ¼ inch (0.6 cm) thick and place in a bowl. Add Hawaiian chilies, garlic, and sea salt. Mix and set aside.

In a spice grinder, grind crushed red pepper, mustard seeds, cumin seeds, fenugreek seeds, cinnamon stick, and black peppercorns to a fairly smooth texture and add to salted limes. Add turmeric, sugar, and lime juice and mix together with your fingers to combine flavors. Cover bowl with a cheesecloth and leave overnight.

The next day, transfer to sterilized jars and refrigerate. Once opened, use in 2 days. Keeps well unopened for 2 to 3 weeks.

Yield: 1 pint (500 ml)

8 large limes

15 Hawaiian chilies

2 garlic cloves, crushed

2 teaspoons (10 ml) sea salt

1 teaspoon (5 ml) crushed red pepper

1 tablespoon (15 m) black mustard seeds

2 teaspoons (10 ml) cumin seeds

½ teaspoon (2.5 ml) fenugreek seeds

1-inch (2.5 cm) piece of cinnamon stick, crushed to bits

½ teaspoon (2.5 cm) black peppercorns

¼ teaspoon (1.25 ml) turmeric

1 tablespoon (15 ml) sugar

½ cup (125 ml) fresh lime or lemon juice

Salted Lemon Wedges

12 large lemons, washed and dried

8 tablespoons (120 ml) kosher salt

3 tablespoons (45 ml) black peppercorns, crushed

10 cardamom pods, crushed

10 whole cloves

2-inch (5 cm) piece of cinnamon stick, crushed into smaller pieces

2 to 3 cups (500 to 750 ml) vegetable oil

Pickled lemons are addictive. They are so exotic, no matter how you use them. I like to roast whole fish with pickled lemons, onion wedges, hot green chilies, and tomato wedges. It is an easy and delicious way of preparing fish. I often add pickled lemons—sliced, chopped, or in wedges—along with spices when roasting lamb or chicken. Keep this pickle handy. It is also a lovely addition to a simple hors d'oeuvres platter.

Directions

Cut lemons in half lengthwise, then cut each half into 4 wedges. Place in a large nonreactive bowl, add salt, and mix thoroughly. Cover and let sit for 2 days.

Place lemons in a strainer to drain. Discard liquid. Transfer lemon wedges to a sterilized jar and distribute the spices evenly on lemons. Pour oil over lemons and seal the jar tightly. Refrigerate for 4 weeks before using.

Yield: about 2 pints (1 L)

Pickled Grape Tomatoes

This is a versatile accompaniment. Serve with broiled or grilled sea-food and vegetables such as grilled squash, cooked greens, steamed green beans, and asparagus.

Directions

Place tomatoes, lemon rind, and dill in a sterilized jar. Place ginger, vinegar, white wine, sugar, and peppercorns in a pan over low heat and simmer for 10 minutes. Season with salt to taste and pour over tomatoes. Cool, cover jar, and refrigerate. Use after 2 days.

Yield: 1 pint (500 ml)

1 pound (453 g) grape tomatoes, washed and dried

Rind of 1 lemon

¼ cup (60 ml) fresh dill sprigs

½-inch (1.25 cm) piece of ginger, thinly sliced

½ cup (125 ml) vinegar

1 cup (250 ml) white wine

1 cup (250 ml) sugar

1 teaspoon (5 ml) black peppercorns

Salt

Pickled Beets

Pickled beets are good in a salad, on an hors d'oeuvres tray, or in a vegetable sandwich. The simple combination of these beets and goat cheese is delicious.

Directions

Place beets and salt in a pan, add cold water to cover, and cook over high heat for about 25 minutes, or until beets are cooked through. Place beets, unpeeled, in a jar and set aside.

Combine vinegar, sugar, ginger powder, coriander seeds, and black peppercorns in a pan, place over high heat, and bring to a boil. Remove from heat and carefully pour liquid over beets. Cover the jar, cool, and refrigerate for 1 week before using. Beets may be eaten peeled or unpeeled.

Yield: 1 pint (500 ml)

1 pound (453 g) baby beets, washed and trimmed to neaten

2 teaspoons (10 ml) salt

1½ cups (375 ml) white wine vinegar

¼ cup (60 ml) sugar

1 teaspoon (5 ml) dried ginger powder

1 teaspoon (5 ml) coriander seeds, lightly crushed

1 teaspoon (5 ml) black peppercorns

Pickled Cherries

1½ pounds (680 g) Bing cherries
with stems, washed

1 cup (250 ml) white wine

1 cup (250 ml) white wine vinegar

2 cups (500 ml) sugar

1 teaspoon (5 ml) black peppercorns

2-inch (5 cm) piece of cinnamon stick

4 cloves

4 cardamom pods

¼ blade of mace

Peel of 1 orange

These gorgeous cherries have a festive aroma, because of the fragrant spices used, and a jar comes in handy during the Christmas season. Use them as an elegant garnish for roast pork on your holiday table, in sauces, or as an accent on an hors d'oeuvres tray.

Directions

Sort cherries and place in a sterilized jar.

Put remaining ingredients in a pan and bring to a simmer over low heat. Simmer for 10 minutes. Remove and discard orange peel and pour syrup over cherries. Cool, cover jar, and refrigerate for 3 weeks before using.

Yield: 1½ pints (750 ml)

Pickled Grapes

1½ (680 g) pounds seedless red grapes,
stems removed

8 ounces (226 g) granulated sugar, or
to taste

8 ounces (226 g) white balsamic vinegar

2-inch (5 cm) piece of cinnamon stick

1-inch (1.25 cm) blade of mace

Salt

Pickled grapes, like pickled cherries, make a lovely garnish.

Directions

Wash grapes and dry on paper towels. Place in a glass container.

Add remaining ingredients to a nonreactive saucepan and season with salt to taste. Place pan over moderate heat and bring mixture to a simmer. Simmer for 5 minutes, then pour over grapes. Cool. Cover and refrigerate overnight. Use within 1 or 2 days.

Yield: 1 pint (500 ml)

"Sinhala Achaharu"

Water for blanching vegetables

Salt

30 small shallots

20 green chilies (such as serrano chilies), stems trimmed

1 carrot, peeled and thinly sliced, about ½ cup (125 ml)

6 green beans, cut into 2-inch (5 cm) lengths

½ cup (125 ml) peeled and thinly sliced green papaya

3 cups apple cider vinegar

4 dried red chilies

½ cup (125 ml) black mustard seeds, coarsely ground

1 tablespoon (15 ml) ground cumin

1 tablespoon (15 ml) minced ginger

6 garlic cloves, minced

1 tablespoon (15 ml) black pepper

½ teaspoon (2.5 ml) turmeric

4-inch (10 cm) piece of cinnamon stick

1 tablespoon (15 ml) freshly grated horseradish

1 tablespoon (15 ml) sugar

This is a favorite Sri Lankan pickle. Traditionally, coconut vinegar is used for pickling, but cider vinegar is a good substitute if coconut vinegar is not available. The large amount of ground black mustard seeds creates a rich, thick pickling mix.

Directions

In a medium pot, bring water to a boil with 1 teaspoon (5 ml) salt. Add shallots and green chilies and cook for 1 minute, then strain vegetables and place on paper towels. Set pot aside.

In the same pot, add fresh water and another teaspoon (5 ml) of salt, and bring to a boil. Add carrots, beans, and green papaya, cook for 1 minute, then strain and place on paper towels to dry.

Transfer shallots, green chilies, carrots, beans, and papaya to a large bowl.

In a small pan, heat vinegar with red chilies and ground mustard seeds over low heat and simmer for 3 minutes. Remove from heat and leave to soak for a few minutes.

In a blender, grind the vinegar-soaked chilies and mustard seeds, cumin, ginger, and garlic to a smooth paste and pour over vegetable mixture in the bowl. Add black pepper, turmeric, cinnamon stick, horseradish, and sugar with salt to taste. Using a sterilized spoon, mix thoroughly.

Transfer to a sterilized jar, cover, and refrigerate for 3 days before using. Keeps well for 1 or 2 months.

Yield: 3 pints (1.5 L)

Cucumber Pickles

Use these pickles with grilled or barbecued meat and seafood, as part of a vegetable platter, and in salads. They add a special crunch and taste to sandwiches and are a convenient snack as well.

Directions

Cut cucumber into ½-inch (1.25 cm) cubes. (You'll need about 2 cups [500 ml].) Place in a medium nonreactive bowl, sprinkle with salt, and set aside for 1 hour.

To make the seasoning liquid, place vinegar, mustard, pepper, dill seeds, ginger, and garlic in another medium nonreactive bowl and mix thoroughly.

Drain cucumber in a colander and gently press out excess water. Fold cucumbers into the seasoning liquid. Transfer to a jar, cover, and refrigerate.

Yield: 1 pint (500 ml)

2 unpeeled cucumbers, halved lengthwise and seeded

1 tablespoon (15 ml) salt

1½ cups (375 ml) white wine vinegar

2 tablespoons (30 ml) Dijon grainy mustard

1 teaspoon (5 ml) black pepper

1 teaspoon (5 ml) dill seeds

1 teaspoon (5 ml) minced ginger

1 teaspoon (5 ml) minced garlic

Spicy Pickles

There are many ways of using these pickles. Chop and use as toppings for meat-based hors d'oeuvres or canapés, or serve them in a bowl on a crudité platter.

Directions

Place cucumbers in a large bowl and add cold water to cover. Add salt and let stand overnight.

The next day, strain cucumbers and rinse in cold water. Transfer to jars along with onions, red and green chilies, garlic, and dill sprigs.

In a 2-quart pot, combine vinegar with dill seeds and black peppercorns over medium heat. Bring to a boil, then pour mixture over cucumber mixture. Cover jars, cool, and refrigerate.

Yield: 4 pints (2 L)

2½ pounds (1.13 kg) small pickling cucumbers

¼ cup (60 ml) salt

3 small red onions, cut into ⅛-inch (0.31 cm) slices

4 small fresh hot red chilies

4 small fresh hot green chilies

4 garlic cloves, peeled and quartered lengthwise

1¼ cups (310 ml) fresh dill sprigs

1½ quarts (1.5 L) apple cider vinegar

1 tablespoon (15 ml) dill seeds

1 tablespoon (15 ml) black peppercorns

Jaggery Pickles with Fruit and Dates

Jaggery pickles are a delicious accompaniment to roast or grilled pork or baked pork chops. They are also a reliable partner in festive rice and curry menus. If jaggery is not available, you may substitute brown sugar.

Directions

Wash and dry yellow wax peppers. Trim each pepper, halve lengthwise, remove seeds, and cut into ½-inch (1.25 cm) pieces. Place in a medium nonreactive bowl and set aside.

Repeat with Anaheim chilies and add to the peppers in the bowl.

Add onion, carrots, dates, and pineapple to the peppers and chilies in the bowl.

In a nonreactive medium pan, add remaining ingredients over low heat and season with salt to taste. Bring to a slow simmer, then turn heat to medium and bring to a boil. Pour over vegetables and fruit in the bowl and mix well to combine flavors.

Cool and transfer to a sterilized jar. Refrigerate for 24 hours before using. Keeps for 1 week.

Yield: 1 pint (500 ml)

4 yellow wax peppers

4 green Anaheim chilies

1 red onion, cut into ½-inch (1.25 cm) cubes

1 medium carrot, trimmed, peeled, and cut into ½-inch (1.25 cm) cubes

¼ pound (113 g) pitted dates, diced large

1 cup (250 ml) pineapple chunks

2 tablespoons (30 ml) Dijon grainy mustard

1 teaspoon (5 ml) cayenne pepper

½ teaspoon (2.5 ml) black pepper

½ teaspoon (2.5 ml) ground cumin

2 cups (500 ml) apple cider vinegar

¼ pound (113 g) grated jaggery

Salt

Fast Pickled Fruit

2 pounds (907 g) watermelon, cut off
the rind and seeded

½ small honeydew melon, cut off
the rind and seeded

1 cantaloupe, cut off the rind and seeded

2 cups (500 ml) sugar

½ cup (125 ml) distilled vinegar

1 cup (250 ml) white wine

1 cup (250 ml) water

5 whole cloves

1 bay leaf

2-inch (5 cm) piece of cinnamon stick

This fruit pickle is easy to make and has to be used within a day or two, before the melons lose their beautiful colors. Serve with roast ham and, of course, mustard. The pickles will look better if you use a melon baller, but they will be just as delicious if the melons are cut into large dice.

Directions

Using a melon baller, scoop out melon balls and place in a deep glass bowl or dish. (You'll need 4 cups [1 L].)

In a medium nonreactive pan, add sugar, vinegar, white wine, water, cloves, bay leaf, and cinnamon stick over low heat and simmer for 20 minutes. Remove from heat and cool.

Pour spiced syrup over fruit. Cover dish and refrigerate overnight. Serve fruit with syrup, avoiding spices. Keeps well for 2 days.

Yield: 2½ pints (1.25 L)

Fast Mustard Pickles

These pickles are a great addition to a Thanksgiving or Christmas table. The sour and sweet pickles are an appropriate companion for rich, fatty food. These pickles must be used up fast!

Directions

Place apricots, dates, pineapple, carrots, and red onion in a glass dish. Mix remaining ingredients together with salt to taste and pour over fruits and vegetables. Mix thoroughly to combine. Cover tightly and refrigerate for 2 days before using. Keeps for a few days.

Yield: 1 pint (500 ml)

½ cup (125 ml) finely chopped dried apricots

½ cup (125 ml) chopped, seeded dates

1 cup (250 ml) medium-diced pineapple

½ cup (125 ml) medium-diced carrots

½ cup (125 ml) medium-diced red onion

1 cup (250 ml) apple cider vinegar

1 cup (250 ml) white wine

2 tablespoons (30 ml) Dijon grainy mustard

2 tablespoons (30 ml) sugar

1 tablespoon (15 ml) dried ginger powder

¼ teaspoon (1.25 ml) turmeric

1 teaspoon (5 ml) black pepper

Salt

Sweet Citrus Pickles

Sweet citrus pickles are a lively addition to the Christmas table along with any other pickles or chutneys you have on hand. Serve them all in dainty glass dishes!

Directions

Cut lemons, oranges, and limes into quarters and remove and discard seeds. Place in a bowl and mix in salt. Cover and refrigerate for 4 days, turning fruit daily so the salt is evenly distributed.

Strain fruit and discard juice. Place prepared fruit in a medium heavy-bottomed saucepan. Add ginger, mustard seeds, cayenne pepper, cinnamon stick, vinegar, and sugar. Simmer over low heat until the mixture thickens, about 35 minutes. Cool and store for 1 week before serving.

Yield: 1 pint (500 ml)

6 lemons

1 orange

2 limes

2 tablespoons (30 ml) salt

¼ cup (60 ml) minced ginger

1 teaspoon (5 ml) crushed black mustard seeds

1 teaspoon (5 ml) cayenne pepper

4-inch (10 cm) piece of cinnamon stick

1 pint (500 ml) apple cider vinegar

1½ cups (375 ml) light brown sugar

Stuffed Pickled Wax Peppers

Many people, especially those who are used to exotic tastes, love these hot and pungent pickles. One of my favorite ways to use them is to roast a whole fish, flavored with spices, add a few stuffed pickled peppers around the fish when it is almost done, then serve it with a luscious fresh yogurt sauce.

Directions

Make a cut lengthwise in the side of each pepper and remove seeds, leaving stem intact. In a medium pan, bring water to a boil. Add peppers and cook for 1 minute. Drain in a colander and refresh with cold water. Place the colander with the peppers over a bowl and let peppers drain well.

In a bowl, combine mustard, black pepper, curry powder, sugar, ginger, garlic, and ½ cup (125 ml) of the vinegar with a pinch of salt. Whisk until smooth to make the seasoning mix.

In a bowl, combine the grated papaya and about 2 to 3 tablespoons (30 to 40 ml) of the seasoning mix. Mix well. Taste and add more seasoning mix if needed.

Stuff peppers with the seasoned papaya and place them in a sterilized jar. Add the remaining seasoning mix to the rest of the vinegar and pour over the stuffed peppers. Refrigerate for 3 days before using. Keeps well for 1 week.

Yield: 1 pint (500 ml)

12 yellow wax peppers with stems

3 cups (750 ml) water

2 tablespoons (30 ml) Dijon grainy mustard

2 teaspoons (10 ml) black pepper

1 teaspoon (5 ml) curry powder

1 teaspoon (5 ml) sugar

1 tablespoon (15 ml) minced ginger

6 garlic cloves, minced into a smooth paste

1½ cups (375 ml) white wine vinegar, or more if needed

Salt

1 cup (250 ml) grated green papaya

Pickled Cauliflower

1 medium cauliflower

1 cup (250 ml) apple cider vinegar

¼ cup (60 ml) plus 1 tablespoon (15 ml) brown sugar

1 tablespoon (15 ml) curry powder

¼ cup (60 ml) water

1 teaspoon (5 ml) black pepper

Salt

1 tablespoon (15 ml) olive oil

For this preparation, the cauliflower florets are roasted after they are briefly pickled. The result is a zesty, spicy accompaniment to rice, fish, chicken, or meat.

Directions

Trim cauliflower and cut into 1-inch (2.5 cm) florets. Set aside.

In a saucepan, combine vinegar, ¼ cup (60 ml) brown sugar, curry powder, water, and pepper and season with salt to taste. Simmer for 5 minutes and pour into a shallow, wide dish. Add cauliflower and stir to coat with seasonings. Refrigerate overnight.

The next day, preheat oven to 350°F (176°C).

Strain cauliflower and transfer to a baking pan lined with parchment paper. Combine the 1 tablespoon (15 ml) brown sugar and olive oil and coat cauliflower with mixture. Roast for about 35 minutes. When done, cauliflower should be speckled with a golden color. Serve hot or at room temperature.

Yield: 2 to 2½ cups (500 to 625 ml)

Ripe Mango Pickles

These delicious mango pickles can be used as an accompaniment to roasted meats and barbecued poultry or as a sauce for sautéed or grilled seafood.

Directions

Cut mangoes into ½-inch (1.25 cm) cubes. (You'll need 2 cups [500 ml]).

Add vinegar, wine, sugar, cinnamon, and cloves to a small nonreactive pan over low heat and cook for about 10 minutes, until the syrup is thick. Add mangoes, lemon juice, and a pinch of salt and simmer for 8 minutes, until mangoes turn transparent. Add chilies and remove from heat. Cool. Transfer to a sterilized jar and refrigerate.

Yield: 1 pint (500 ml)

2 ripe, firm mangoes, peeled and seeded

½ cup (125 ml) white wine vinegar

½ cup (125 ml) white wine

1½ cups (375 ml) sugar

4-inch (10 cm) piece of cinnamon stick

6 whole cloves

1 tablespoon (15 ml) lemon juice

Salt

4 fresh red chilies, with stems

Indian Green Mango Pickles

Mangoes should be young and tender for pickling, so that it is easy to cut through their seeds. Use with rice and curry meals.

Directions

Trim mangoes and halve them, cutting through the seeds. Remove and discard seeds, then cut each half into four pieces. (You'll need 2 cups of prepared mangoes.)

Add oil to a heavy pan or skillet over moderate heat. Add peppercorns, mustard seeds, fennel seeds, and cumin seeds. Cook for 5 minutes and add crushed red pepper, turmeric, asafetida, and salt to taste. Stir in mangoes and remove from heat.

Transfer to a glass bowl and cover loosely with cheesecloth. Leave in the hot sun or a warm place during the day and move to the refrigerator by evening. Repeat for 5 to 6 days. Mangoes should be tender by then. Transfer to sterilized jars, cover, and refrigerate for 2 to 3 days before using.

Yield: 2 pints (1 L)

12 green mangoes, unpeeled

1½ cups (375 ml) vegetable oil

2 tablespoons (30 ml) coarsely crushed black peppercorns

2 tablespoons (30 ml) coarsely crushed black mustard seeds

1 tablespoon (15 ml) coarsely crushed fennel seeds

1 tablespoon (15 ml) crushed cumin seeds

2 tablespoons (30 ml) crushed red pepper

2 teaspoons (10 ml) turmeric

½ teaspoon (2.5 ml) asafetida

1 tablespoon (15 ml) salt

Green Mango Pickles

2 large mature mangoes, peeled and seeded

1 tablespoon (15 ml) crushed red pepper

1 teaspoon (5 ml) ground black pepper

1 teaspoon (5 ml) ground cumin

1 tablespoon (15 ml) Dijon grainy mustard

½ cup (125 ml) apple cider vinegar

2 tablespoons (30 ml) sugar

Salt

During the summer in Sri Lanka, mango trees are laden with fruit. People there prepare mangoes in many different ways. Green mango pickles are an all-around favorite, especially with young adults. Mango season coincides with school vacations. On lazy hot afternoons, we used to prepare our own pickles for snacking. The fun part is pounding the pickles to blend the pungent spices into the fresh mango. Hawaiian mangoes are fleshy and crunchy and make good pickles.

Directions

Cut mangoes into slices ¼ inch (0.6 cm) thick and place in a wooden bowl. (You'll need 2 cups [500 ml].) The slices will be uneven but attractive.

Add remaining ingredients to the mangoes and mix, seasoning with salt to taste. With a mortar and pestle, pound the mango slices briefly, bruising the fruit, to help it absorb the seasoning. (Alternately, use a clean hand and mix with force, almost crushing the mangoes, so the seasoning gets into the fruit.) Transfer to a glass dish and refrigerate. Serve chilled.

Yield: 1 pint (500 ml)

Maui Onion Pickles

3 pounds (1.36 kg) Maui onions, peeled, trimmed, and washed

2 pints (1 L) distilled vinegar

4 2-inch (5 cm) pieces of cinnamon stick

4 bay leaves

12 ripe fresh chilies, with stems

1 tablespoon (15 ml) black peppercorns

1 teaspoon (5 ml) whole cloves

1½ cups (375 ml) sugar, or to taste

Salt

Sweet and crunchy Maui onions are the best onions for pickling. These pickles are good in salads and as an accompaniment to grilled and roasted meat alongside creamed horseradish.

Directions

Wipe off any moisture on the onions with paper towels. Cut each onion into 6 wedges and place wedges in sterilized jars.

In a pan, combine vinegar, cinnamon, bay leaves, chilies, black peppercorns, cloves, and sugar with salt to taste. Place over high heat and boil steadily for 5 minutes. Pour immediately into jars, making sure spices are divided equally among jars and liquid covers onions.

Cover jars, cool, and refrigerate for 2 weeks, shaking jars twice a day. Use after 2 weeks.

Yield: 4 pints (2 L)

Onion and Chili Pickles

½ pound (226 g) small shallots, trimmed, washed, and wiped dry

25 green serrano chilies with stems, washed and wiped dry

3 cups (750 ml) distilled vinegar

1 tablespoon (15 ml) sugar

1 teaspoon (5 ml) black peppercorns

1 teaspoon (5 ml) crushed cumin seeds

2-inch (5 cm) piece of cinnamon stick

Salt

Vegetarians love a bowl of pickles with rice and vegetable curry. Take these pickles on a picnic and serve with barbecued chicken or ribs.

Directions

Place shallots in a jar. Trim serrano chilies, cut slits on the sides, and add to the shallots.

Place vinegar, sugar, black peppercorns, cumin seeds, and cinnamon stick in a pan over low heat and season with salt to taste. Bring to a boil. Pour mixture over shallots and chilies. Cool, cover, and refrigerate for 4 days, shaking jar every day, before using.

Yield: 2 pints (1 L)

Pickled Red Onion Rings

2 red onions

1 cup (250 ml) red wine vinegar

¼ cup (60 ml) red wine

¾ cup (180 ml) sugar

1 bay leaf

1-inch (2.5 cm) piece of cinnamon stick

½ teaspoon (2.5 ml) black peppercorns

Salt

These pickled onion rings are a complement to pork dishes. For a piquant punch, I add them to simple greens and garden salads. Use some pickling juice in the dressing. It is sour! The red wine vinegar and red wine in the pickling liquid turn the onion rings an attractive burgundy color. White onions are also suitable for this recipe; pickling will turn white onion rings a pale rosy color.

Directions

Cut onions crosswise into slices ¼ inch (0.6 cm) thick, then separate slices into rings and place in a sterilized jar. Boil vinegar, wine, sugar, bay leaf, cinnamon, and black peppercorns with salt to taste. Pour over onion rings and let onion rings cool in brining mix.

When cool, cover and refrigerate. Use after 2 days.

Yield: 1 pint (500 ml)

Pickled Whole Onions

1½ pounds (680 g) pearl onions

3 cups (750 ml) water

¼ cup (60 ml) salt

¾ cup (180 ml) sugar

2½ cups (625 ml) distilled vinegar

1 bay leaf

1 teaspoon (5 ml) black peppercorns

1 teaspoon (5 ml) whole cloves

2-inch (5 cm) piece of cinnamon stick

Add a bowl of pickled onions to a vegetable platter, or use as a garnish for roasted meat. Toss in hot butter, add chopped chives, and serve as a garnish for sautéed fish.

Directions

Trim and peel onions and place in a bowl. Bring water and salt to a fast boil and pour over onions. Let sit overnight.

The next day, place onions in a strainer and drain liquid into a bowl. Discard liquid.

Combine sugar, vinegar, bay leaf, black peppercorns, cloves, and cinnamon stick in a pan. Place over medium heat and bring to a slow simmer. Cook for 5 minutes, then add onions and simmer for 2 minutes, until onions are half cooked and translucent. Transfer to jars. Cool, cover, and refrigerate for 3 days before using.

Yield: 2 pints (1 L)

Bitter Melon Pickles

A few slices of pickled bitter melon are a great addition to a fresh tomato and red onion salad. Or sauté quickly with sliced onion and chopped tomato and serve with rice and sautéed fish. Understandably, bitter melon is not a favorite with most people, but those who love it look for unusual ways of preparing it.

Directions

Slice bitter melon lengthwise. Remove and discard seeds only if they are hard. Slice melon about 1/8 inch (0.3 cm) thick. Place in a dish.

In a blender, grind mustard seeds, chilies, ginger, cloves, and turmeric with vinegar. Pour mixture over the bitter melon and season very lightly with salt to taste. Mix to combine and refrigerate for 3 days before using.

Yield: 1 pint (500 ml)

1 pound (453 g) bitter melon

½ cup (125 ml) black mustard seeds

4 dried red chilies

½-inch (1.25 cm) piece of ginger

4 garlic cloves

½ teaspoon (2.5 ml) turmeric

2 cups (500 ml) distilled vinegar

Salt

Pickled Okra

Okra, native to Africa, is one of those vegetables that people either like or hate. Many are put off by its main characteristic, a mucilaginous quality. Pick small to medium okra that are not discolored. Thick, large okra with seeds protruding under their skins are coarse and fibrous. Pickled okra may be used cut up or whole. Okra does well with tomatoes in a salad or with other pickled counterparts such as olives, peppers, and onions on an hors d'oeuvres tray.

Directions

Wash okra and leave on paper towels to dry, then place in a sterilized jar along with lemon slices.

Combine remaining ingredients in a small pan over low heat, add salt to taste, and simmer for 5 minutes. Pour contents of pan over okra and lemon slices, cover jar, and let cool completely, then refrigerate 1 week before using.

Yield: 2 pints (1 L)

15 to 20 medium okra, stems trimmed and discarded

12 lemon slices

1½ cups (375 ml) white wine

½ cup (125 ml) rice wine vinegar

½ cup (125 ml) sugar

1 teaspoon (5 ml) whole cloves

2-inch (5 cm) piece of cinnamon stick

1 teaspoon (5 ml) black peppercorns

1 teaspoon (5 ml) crushed red pepper

Kosher salt

Pickled Stuffed Dates

Dates are the fruit of the date palm tree. Varieties of dates are readily available. Plump and shiny medjool dates are excellent for stuffing. Pickled dates pair well with salty blue cheese and are a wonderful addition to the cheese platter.

Directions

Make a cut on one side of each date, then remove and discard seed. Stuff dates with chopped almonds, then place in a sterilized jar.

Boil the remaining ingredients with salt to taste. Set aside for 5 minutes, then pour the hot spiced vinegar over the dates. Cover tightly and shake jar to make sure all the dates are submerged. Uncover jar and let cool. When cool, cover jar, and refrigerate for 4 weeks before using.

Yield: 1½ pints (750 ml)

1½ pounds (680 g) dates

½ pound (226 g) roasted almonds, coarsely chopped

2 cups (500 ml) white wine vinegar

1 cup (250 ml) white wine

¼ cup (60 ml) balsamic vinegar

¼ cup (60 ml) sugar

1 teaspoon (5 ml) black pepper

1 teaspoon (5 ml) cayenne pepper

1 teaspoon (5 ml) ground cinnamon

½ teaspoon (2.5 ml) ground cloves

Salt

Pickled Papayas

1 half-ripe papaya, peeled, halved, and seeded

1 cup (250 ml) white wine vinegar

½ cup (125 ml) white wine

1½ cups (375 ml) sugar

2 teaspoons (10 ml) julienned ginger

1 tablespoon (15 ml) chopped lemon rind with white pith

2 sprigs of fresh thyme

1 tablespoon (15 ml) lemon juice

Pickled papayas are so special. Use as part of an appetizer, a garnish for seafood, or a topping for a sweet ice cream.

Directions

Cut papaya into ½-inch (1.25 cm) cubes. (You'll need 2 cups [500 ml].)

Place vinegar, wine, sugar, ginger, lemon rind, and thyme in a non-reactive pan over medium heat. Cook, stirring, for about 10 minutes, until syrup is thick. Add papaya and lemon juice and simmer 10 minutes, until papaya turns transparent. Remove and discard thyme.

Papaya is delicate, so shake the pan, instead of stirring its contents, from this point onward, to avoid breaking up papaya. Cook for 2 to 3 minutes. Cool. Transfer to a sterilized jar and refrigerate.

Yield: 2½ cups (625 ml)

White Asparagus Vinaigrette

White and green asparagus are excellent dressed in a tart vinaigrette. Serve as an accompaniment to carved ham or prosciutto. By itself, this dish is also a wonderful salad, and it makes a good appetizer for a fine meal.

Directions

In a medium pot, bring water to a boil. Add asparagus and blanch for 3 to 4 minutes. Strain asparagus and place in a bowl of ice water. Drain asparagus and dry on paper towels, place in a dish, and refrigerate.

For the vinaigrette, in a small bowl, whisk together vinegar, lemon juice, mustard, shallots, parsley, and pepper and add salt to taste. Gradually drizzle olive oil into the bowl and continue to whisk until thoroughly combined. Let rest a few hours at room temperature and allow flavors to blend.

Take asparagus out of the refrigerator and spoon vinaigrette over, tossing gently to mix. Serve with carved ham or prosciutto.

6 servings

4 cups (1 L) cold water

1 pound (453 g) asparagus, trimmed and peeled

1 tablespoon (15 ml) sherry vinegar

1 tablespoon (15 ml) lemon juice

1 teaspoon (5 ml) Dijon grainy mustard

1 teaspoon (5 ml) minced shallots

1 teaspoon (5 ml) chopped parsley or snipped chives

Freshly ground black pepper

Salt

4 tablespoons (60 ml) olive oil

Eggplant "Pahi"

1½ pounds (680 g) eggplants

Salt

1 teaspoon (5 ml) turmeric

¾ cup (180 ml) apple cider vinegar

3 tablespoons (45 ml) black mustard seeds, crushed

1 tablespoon (15 ml) chopped ginger

1 tablespoon (15 ml) chopped garlic

½ cup (125 ml) vegetable oil

1 cup (250 ml) small shallots or halved large shallots

12 fresh red chilies

12 fresh green chilies

2 teaspoons (10 ml) crushed red pepper

1 tablespoon (15 ml) curry powder

1 tablespoon (15 ml) brown sugar

Pahi is a beloved Sri Lankan eggplant dish, a pickle of sorts. This elegant pickle is not only for festive meals; it is prepared often, especially for Sunday lunch. I also serve it as a side dish with lamb.

Directions

Cut each eggplant lengthwise into quarters, then cut quarters in half and slice halves into pieces 2 inches (5 cm) long. Place in a large bowl. Sprinkle with 1 tablespoon (15 ml) salt, mix thoroughly, and set aside for 20 minutes. Rinse eggplant pieces and dry with paper towels. Place in another bowl, add turmeric, and mix to coat pieces.

In a blender , blend vinegar, mustard, ginger, and garlic to a smooth puree. Set aside.

Heat oil in a frying pan over medium heat and fry eggplant in two batches until golden brown and crisp. Place pieces on paper towels when they are done, to soak up excess oil. Transfer to a bowl and set aside.

Add shallots to the same frying pan over medium heat and cook for 3 minutes, just enough to wilt them, then remove and place on paper towels. Transfer to the bowl of eggplant. Similarly fry red and green chilies, drain on paper towels, and transfer to the bowl of shallots and eggplant.

There should be about a teaspoon of oil left in the frying pan. Turn heat to low and add the vinegar mixture, crushed red pepper, curry powder, and sugar. Stir to combine and season with salt to taste. Fold in fried eggplant, shallots, and chilies. Continue to cook over low heat for 2 to 3 minutes, gently turning the vegetables to coat them with seasonings.

Yield: 1½ pints (750 ml)

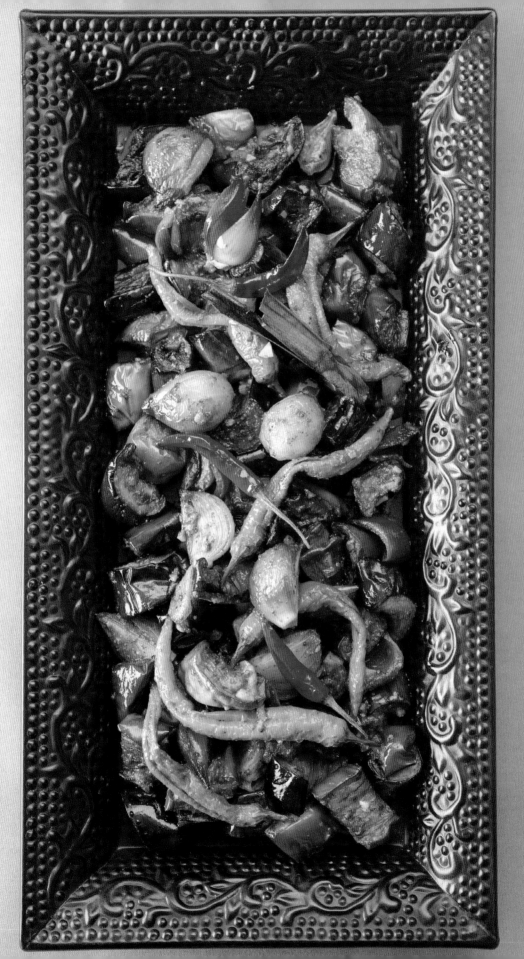

Pineapple Pickles

This quick pickle can be used in many ways. Replace a dressing by spooning it over a vegetable salad or cooked seafood salad. Serve as an accompaniment to a ham or roast. Enrich a ham sandwich, or chop and add to a cream cheese spread. Pineapples vary in sweetness, so adjust sugar accordingly.

Directions

Place the cubed pineapple in a glass or enamel container.

In a blender, blend remaining ingredients with salt to taste. Pour mixture over pineapple and toss to coat. Chill before serving.

Yield: 1 pint (500 ml)

1 pineapple, peeled, cored, and cut into ½-inch (1.25 cm) cubes

1 tablespoon (15 ml) Dijon grainy mustard

1 tablespoon (15 ml) finely minced ginger

1 tablespoon (15 ml) finely minced garlic

½ cup (125 ml) apple cider vinegar

About 2 tablespoons (30 ml) brown sugar, or to taste

1 teaspoon (5 ml) ground black pepper

½ teaspoon (2.5 ml) cayenne pepper

1 teaspoon (5 ml) ground cumin

Salt

Handy Sweet Pickling Syrup

2 cups (500 ml) apple cider vinegar

2 cups (500 ml) white wine vinegar

6 cups (1500 ml) granulated sugar

1 cup (250 ml) light corn syrup

1½ teaspoons (7.5 ml) whole cloves

1-inch (1.25 cm) blade of mace

4-inch (10 cm) piece of cinnamon stick

1 teaspoon (5 ml) cardamom pods

1 teaspoon (5 ml) black peppercorns

1 star anise

1 bay leaf

This is a syrup to have ready to go in the refrigerator. Pour some over raw or poached fruit or vegetables and leave them in the refrigerator to pickle. Fragile fruits such as raspberries and strawberries need no poaching, while firm and fibrous fruits and vegetables may be blanched or poached before being preserved in this syrup. They are all good additions to hors d'oeuvres trays and salads and can also serve as garnishes.

Directions

Place all ingredients in a pan, set pan over moderate heat, and bring to a boil. Continue boiling for 20 minutes.

Cool, strain, and discard all spices but the cinnamon stick. Pour into a jar, cover, and refrigerate. Use as needed.

Yield: 2 pints (1 L)

Sweet Carrot Pickles

These pickles are a colorful addition to an hors d'oeuvres or crudité platter. Add a handful of freshly chopped dill and a spoonful of olive oil to the pickles and serve as a side dish with meat.

½ pound (226 g) peeled sliced carrots

About 1 cup (250 ml) **Handy Sweet Pickling Syrup** (p. 136)

Directions

Place sliced carrots in a dish and pour pickling syrup over carrots, making sure carrots are submerged. Cover dish and refrigerate for 2 to 3 days before using.

Yield: 1 pint (500 ml)

Pickled Radishes

These radishes are lovely on hors d'oeuvres trays and in salads.

1 cup (250 ml) sliced white radishes

About 1½ cups (375 ml) **Handy Sweet Pickling Syrup** (p. 136)

Directions

Place sliced radishes in a jar. Pour pickling syrup over radishes, making sure slices are covered in syrup. Cover dish and let sit for 2 to 3 days before using.

Yield: 1 pint (500 ml)

Pickled Kumquats

3 cups (750 ml) water

1 tablespoon (15 ml) salt

1 pound (453 g) kumquats

2 cups (500 ml) granulated sugar

1 cup (250 ml) white wine vinegar

1 cup (250 ml) white wine

½-inch (1.25 cm) piece of cinnamon stick

1 teaspoon (5 ml) whole cloves

1 teaspoon (5 ml) black pepper

4 cardamom pods, bruised

1 bay leaf

To use pickled kumquats, press out seeds and chop, dice, or cut into strips. Use in sauces, as a garnish, and in compound butter.

Directions

Combine water and salt in a pan and bring to a simmer. Remove from heat, add kumquats, and let stand uncovered for 8 to 10 hours. Transfer kumquats to a colander and let drain, then refresh with cold water and let drain again. With the point of a sharp knife, prick each kumquat in 4 or 5 spots. This will allow the syrup to seep into the kumquats and keep them plump when preserved.

Place sugar, vinegar, wine, spices, and bay leaf in a pan and simmer over low heat for 10 minutes. Add kumquats and simmer for 15 minutes. Remove from heat and leave the kumquats in the syrup overnight.

The next day, transfer kumquats from the pan to a dish and set aside. Place the pan with the syrup over low heat and bring to a simmer. Add kumquats and simmer for 2 minutes. Remove from heat. Cool kumquats and spoon fruit and syrup into sterilized jars. Cover and store for 2 weeks before using.

Yield: 1½ pints (750 ml)

Pickled Pumpkin

Pumpkins are naturally sweet and combine well with mustard, vinegar, and maple syrup or dark brown sugar. They are great for pickling. If you have a choice, use kabocha pumpkin for pickling; it is sweeter than other varieties.

Use as you would any other pickle. Or give it a fancy touch. Sometimes I toss the pickles with a handful of honeyed walnuts and another handful of chopped candied pineapple, especially when the dish is for the family Thanksgiving table.

Directions

Cut pumpkin into ¼-inch (0.6 cm) cubes. (You'll need 1½ pints [750 ml].) Sprinkle salt on pumpkin and mix well. Set aside for 2 hours.

Rinse cubed pumpkin in cold water and drain thoroughly. Wipe dry with paper towels. Pack pumpkin into a sterilized jar with raisins, ginger, and garlic.

Add remaining ingredients to a small pan and whisk to combine mustard with liquids. Simmer mixture over low heat until syrupy, 8 to 10 minutes. Pour syrup over pumpkin, making sure cubes are completely covered. Cool, cover jar, and refrigerate for 1 week, shaking jar once a day, before using.

Yield: 1 quart (1 L)

2 to 3 pounds (907 g to 1.3 kg) pumpkin, peeled and seeded

2 tablespoons (30 ml) salt

1 cup (250 ml) golden raisins

2-inch (5 cm) piece of ginger, thinly sliced

6 garlic cloves, crushed

2 cups (500 ml) apple cider vinegar

1½ cups (375 ml) maple syrup

1 cup (250 ml) orange juice

¼ cup (60 ml) balsamic vinegar

2 tablespoons (30 ml) Dijon grainy mustard

1 teaspoon (5 ml) ground cinnamon

1 teaspoon (5 ml) ground cumin seeds

¼ teaspoon (1.25 ml) grated nutmeg

1 teaspoon (5 ml) ground black pepper

Sweet and Sour Pickled Pears

1½ pounds (680 g) pears (about 3 pears)

Juice of 1 lemon

1½ cups (375 ml) sugar

½ cup (125 ml) white wine vinegar

2-inch (5 cm) piece of cinnamon stick

4 whole cloves

Peel of 1 lemon

Pickled pears are delicious in green salads. Place sliced or diced pears on salad and enhance with a generous sprinkling of goat or feta cheese and chopped toasted almonds or pecans.

Directions

Peel, quarter, and core pears. Place in a bowl of water with lemon juice and set aside.

In a pan, combine remaining ingredients with 1 cup (250 ml) of water, place over low heat, and bring to a slow simmer.

Drain pears and add to simmering sugar syrup. Simmer for 10 minutes, until pears are tender but firm. Remove pears from syrup and spoon into a small bowl.

Cook syrup for 10 more minutes, strain, and pour over pears. Cool, cover the bowl of pears, and refrigerate for 3 days.

On the third day, set a strainer on a bowl and pour the pears into the strainer, letting the syrup drip into the bowl. Return pears to the sterilized jar and pour the collected syrup into a saucepan. Simmer the syrup for 3 minutes, then pour hot syrup over pears. Cool, cover jar, and refrigerate for 1 week before using.

Yield: 2 pints (1 L)

Cinnamon-y Apple Pickles

This apple pickle is an elegant accompaniment to cold meats or roasts. The ground cinnamon gives the pickle an appetizing brown tint. You may use less cinnamon if you prefer a light golden color and only a hint of the cinnamon aroma.

Directions

Wash and dry lemon. Cut into thin slices, remove seeds, and chop the lemon slices roughly.

Combine chopped lemon with vinegar, honey, sugar, wine, and spices over medium heat and simmer for 8 minutes. Add apples, stirring frequently, and simmer for 25 minutes. Cool, transfer to a sterilized jar, cover, and refrigerate. Use the next day.

Yield: 1 pint (500 ml)

1 lemon

¾ cup (180 ml) apple cider vinegar

¼ cup (60 ml) honey

¾ cup (180 ml) sugar

¾ cup (180 ml) white wine

1 teaspoon (5 ml) ground cinnamon

½ teaspoon (2.5 ml) ground cloves

1/8 teaspoon (0.62 ml) grated nutmeg

¾ pound (340 g) green apples, peeled, cored, and cut in wedges (about 1 pint [500 ml])

Wi Apple Pickles

This is a fun pickle that young people love.

Directions

Peel and halve the apples, avoiding the seeds. Remove and discard seeds. Slice fruit 1/8 inch (0.3 cm) thick and place in a bowl. (You'll need 2 cups [500 ml].) Sprinkle with salt, mix, and leave for 5 to 6 hours. Rinse apples with cold water and place in a colander to drain.

In a pan, whisk together vinegar, sugar, ginger, garlic, mustard, cayenne pepper, black pepper, and cinnamon stick. Place over high heat and bring to a boil. Pour over apples. Mix thoroughly and transfer to a jar. Cool, cover, and refrigerate for 1 week before using.

Yield: 1 pint (500 ml)

1 pound (453 g) mature wi apples, peeled

2 tablespoons (30 ml) salt

1½ cups (375 ml) distilled vinegar

½ cup (125 ml) sugar

2 teaspoons (10 ml) minced ginger

2 teaspoons (10 ml) minced garlic

2 tablespoons (30 ml) Dijon grainy mustard

1 teaspoon (5 ml) cayenne pepper

1 teaspoon (5 ml) black pepper

2-inch (5 cm) piece of cinnamon stick, crushed

Pickled Watermelon Rind

1 pound (453 g) watermelon rind, green skin and pink flesh removed

1½ tablespoons (22.5 ml) salt

4 2-inch (5 cm) cinnamon sticks, crushed

2 teaspoons (10 ml) whole cloves

2 teaspoons (10 ml) crushed cardamom pods

3 cups (370 ml) sugar

2 cups (500 ml) water

1 cup (250 ml) distilled vinegar

I give these pickles a quick sauté in olive oil over high heat and use them as a garnish for roast veal loin. They are also good with pork roast.

Directions

Cut watermelon rind into thin strips and place in a big bowl. (You'll need about 3½ cups [875ml].) Add cold water to cover and stir in salt, then cover bowl and leave overnight.

The next day, drain salted water, wash rind in cold water, and place in a pan. Add fresh cold water to cover and simmer over medium heat for 10 minutes. Drain in a colander and rinse in cold water. Set aside.

Tie cinnamon sticks, cloves, and cardamom pods in a sachet.

In a pan, combine sugar, water, vinegar, and the spice sachet. Place over medium heat and bring to a simmer. Add rind and simmer for 35 to 40 minutes, or until the rind is translucent. Cool, remove and discard sachet, and transfer rind to sterilized jar. Cover and refrigerate.

Yield: 1 pint (500 ml)

Pickled Plums

Pickled plums are unusual yet delightful when chopped and served with ice cream. Keep in mind that the plums are pickled with their seeds. You may also add plums to demi-glace-based sauces. They will enrich the taste and give body to sauces served with rich meat. I also arrange them whole around a pork roast.

Directions

With the point of a sharp knife, prick each plum in 4 or 5 places.

Combine sugar, water, vinegar, and wine in a straight-sided medium sauté pan. Add spices, place pan over medium heat, and simmer for 15 minutes, until the mixture becomes a shiny syrup. Add plums and simmer 10 minutes, skimming off the foam that floats to the top. With a skimmer, remove plums and set aside. Discard bay leaves.

Bring pan of syrup to a boil over medium heat. Remove from heat, add plums, and cover. Cool and refrigerate overnight.

The next day, place the pan of plums and syrup over medium heat and boil for 5 minutes. Remove plums and set aside, then boil syrup for 5 minutes. Return plums to the hot syrup. Cool, cover, and let sit for 24 hours. Transfer plums and syrup to sterilized jars and refrigerate for 3 weeks before using.

Yield: 3 pints (1½ L)

2 pounds (680 g) small purple plums (about 15 plums), washed and stems removed

4 cups (1 L) sugar

2 cups (500 ml) water

2 cups (500 ml) vinegar

1 cup (250 ml) red wine

2-inch (5 cm) piece of cinnamon stick

1 teaspoon (5 ml) whole cloves

2 bay leaves

SPICY FRUIT SAMBAL

OKRA SAMBAL

"POL" SAMBAL

ROASTED COCONUT SAMBAL

ZUCCHINI "MALLUN"

"BLACHAN"

GREEN CHILI AND COCONUT SAMBAL

HOT CHILI SAMBAL

DEVILED POTATOES

CARROT SAMBAL

PARSLEY SAMBAL

PENNYWORT "GOTUKOLA" SAMBAL

"KUNI" SAMBAL

"SERUNDENG"

"SEENI" SAMBAL

SPICY "CHUTNEY" POWDER

EASY FLAVOR SPRINKLER

CURRY LEAF SAMBAL

LIME PICKLE SAMBAL

BANANA BLOSSOM SAMBAL

FRIED EGGPLANT AND CASHEW SAMBAL

FRIED BITTER MELON SAMBAL

BITTER MELON SAMBAL

LEEK AND TOMATO SAMBAL

COCONUT "MALLUN"

HONEY ROASTED BABY CARROTS

CURRIED PINEAPPLE

CURRIED MANGOES

ROASTED EGGPLANT SAMBAL

SAMBALS

Sambals are exotic accompaniments to main dishes, appetizers, and snacks and are also served as appetizers. Some sambals, like **Spicy Fruit Sambal** (p. 148), are also referred to as relishes, because, it is said, they are so tasty and are "relished" by those who eat them. They are fiery hot, rich, and aromatic or pungent, sweet, tart, or salty, and they spice up any meal they accompany. These are features that set them apart. They have no Western equivalents.

The best sambals come from Sri Lanka, Malaysia, and Indonesia, particularly from Jakarta and the surrounding islands. In these places, any of a variety of fiery sambals are an integral part of a meal. They provide flavor contrasts to the dishes they accompany. In Sri Lanka, a simple rice and curry meal, especially if the curry is mild, has sambal to give it character, a kick to the whole meal. The fierce **Hot Chili Sambal** (p. 159) and others like it generally are produced in small quantities because of their strong taste.

Sambals may be cooked or uncooked and range from simple and fresh to fancy and exotic sambals that take a long time to prepare. Grated fresh coconut is often a main ingredient. Some uncooked sambals that are similar to salads are enriched with grated fresh coconut or thick coconut milk. Taste enhancers commonly used in sambals include dried or fresh whole red chilies or green chilies, onions, ginger, garlic, spices, nuts, and fresh or dried fruit. Fruit juices, tamarind, honey, and vinegars are also favorite seasonings. Seafood products, such as Maldive fish, dried shrimp, and fish sauce, as well as jaggery also give certain dishes unique umami flavors. When preparing and storing sambals, use nonreactive equipment and utensils.

Spicy Fruit Sambal

1 cup (250 ml) small-diced pineapple

½ cup (125 ml) small-diced cantaloupe

½ cup (125 ml) peeled, seeded, small-diced cucumber

¼ cup (60 ml) chopped onion

1 tablespoon (15 ml) shrimp paste

2 fresh red chilies, finely minced

1 tablespoon (15 ml) sugar

1 teaspoon (5 ml) fish sauce

2 tablespoons (30 ml) lime juice, or to taste

Salt

This fruit sambal is an outstanding appetizer, delicious and spicy. It is easily put together and will get your guests ready for the meal to follow.

Directions

Place pineapple, cantaloupe, cucumber, and onion in a dish. Add shrimp paste, chilies, sugar, and fish sauce with lime juice and salt to taste. Mix thoroughly. Serve in a glass bowl at room temperature.

6 servings

Okra Sambal

Okra sambal may be served as a little salad or appetizer before dinner. It may also accompany a rice and curry meal. Occasionally I serve these salad-like sambals as vegetable accompaniments to a roast whole fish or with a platter of grilled seafood. Pick tender young okra for this sambal. They cook faster than overmature okra.

Directions

Heat grill or heat a cast iron skillet on the stove.

Wash okra and trim stems and tails. Cut lengthwise into thin strips, place in a medium bowl, and toss gently in 1 teaspoon (5 ml) salt, 1 teaspoon (5 ml) of the lemon juice (reserve remaining lemon juice), and vegetable oil. Grill the strips of okra, just enough to make marks. (If using a skillet, cook a handful at a time, to avoid overcrowding.)

Place in a medium bowl, add remaining ingredients, and toss. Season with reserved lemon juice and salt to taste. Arrange on a platter and serve.

8 servings

1 pound (453 g) okra

Salt

Juice of 1 large lemon

1 tablespoon (15 ml) vegetable oil

½ cup (125 ml) thinly sliced onion

1 cup (250 ml) halved grape tomatoes or tomatoes of your choice

2 jalapeños, sliced

2 yellow peppers, seeded and cut into thin strips

½ cup (125 ml) chopped dill

1 tablespoon (15 ml) black pepper

1 teaspoon (5 ml) crushed red pepper

1 tablespoon (15 ml) ground Maldive fish or fish sauce to taste

"Pol" Sambal

2 cups (500 ml) grated fresh coconut*

2 teaspoons (10 ml) cayenne pepper

1 tablespoon (15 ml) coarsely ground Maldive fish (optional)

¼ cup (60 ml) chopped onion

3 tablespoons (45 ml) lime juice, or to taste

2 teaspoons (10 ml) salt

*If fresh coconut is not available, substitute 1 cup (250 ml) of unsweetened dried coconut soaked for a few minutes in ¼ cup (60 ml) coconut milk or milk. Before using, gently press out excess liquid from rehydrated coconut.

"Pol sambal" means "coconut sambal." This condiment is almost exclusive to Sri Lanka and is known as its national condiment. Use as an accompaniment to rice and curries. Young Sri Lankan adults love this as a sandwich spread, especially on buttered bread. Pol sambal is equally good made without Maldive fish.

Directions

Place ingredients in a food processor and blend to combine flavors. Taste and season with more lime juice and salt if needed. Spoon into a medium serving dish and serve at room temperature.

6 to 8 servings

Roasted Coconut Sambal

1 cup (250 ml) grated fresh or dried grated coconut

4 dried red chilies, seeded and broken into small pieces

¼ cup (60 ml) chopped shallots

1 teaspoon (5 ml) chopped garlic

2 tablespoons (30 ml) coarsely ground Maldive fish (optional)

4 tablespoons (60 ml) lime or lemon juice

Salt

Grated fresh or dried grated coconut may be used for this special sambal. Dried coconut is preferable because it will brown more quickly. Hot dried chilies and their seeds give this dish its essential heat, a characteristic of sambal. This sambal commonly accompanies a rice and curry meal. Vegetarians love it, and it is equally good without Maldive fish.

Directions

Place a cast iron skillet over moderate heat, and when skillet is hot, add coconut. Using a wooden spoon, stir constantly and roast to a deep brown color. Add chilies and stir to brown them.

Remove skillet from heat and transfer coconut and chilies to a blender. Add shallots, garlic, and Maldive fish (if using) with lemon juice and salt to taste and blend to a smooth paste. Mound on a small glass dish and serve at room temperature.

4 to 8 servings

Zucchini "Mallun"

"Mallun" refers to a cooking technique in which shredded leafy green vegetables are cooked briefly in a clay pot. Zucchini is bland and very predictable. The seasonings used in this recipe transform the vegetable into an exotic palate pleaser very different from plain sautéed or steamed zucchini. I use this technique, which does not require oil, with a few other vegetables as well.

Directions

Cut each zucchini in half lengthwise, then halve each piece lengthwise again. Cut pieces into ¼-inch (0.6 cm) dice. (You'll need about 2 cups [500 ml].) Add water to the zucchini and set aside.

In a food processor or a blender, grind coconut, shallots, green chili, garlic, ginger, curry leaves, mustard, cumin, black pepper, and turmeric to a coarse paste. Set aside.

Place a wide medium sauté pan over high heat. Add zucchini, stirring with a wooden spoon, and cook briefly for a 3 or 4 minutes. The zucchini should still be crunchy. Add reserved seasoning paste and mix briskly into cooked zucchini. Add salt to taste and continue cooking, stirring, for 3 to 4 minutes. Transfer to a medium dish, top with diced tomatoes, and serve hot.

6 servings

2 zucchini, washed, stems and tails trimmed

2 tablespoons (30 ml) water

½ cup (125 ml) grated fresh coconut

1 medium shallot, sliced

1 green chili, sliced

2 garlic cloves, chopped

1 teaspoon (5 ml) minced ginger

10 curry leaves

1 tablespoon (15 ml) Dijon grainy mustard

1 teaspoon (5 ml) ground cumin

1 teaspoon (5 ml) black pepper

¼ teaspoon (1.25 ml) turmeric

Salt

1 medium tomato, diced small

"Blachan"

½ cup (125 ml) dried shrimp

¼ cup (60 ml) unsweetened, dried shredded coconut

6 whole dried red chilies, stems removed

¼ cup (60 ml) sliced shallots

2 teaspoons (10 ml) minced ginger

1 teaspoon (5 ml) minced garlic

¼ cup (60 ml) coconut milk

1 teaspoon (5 ml) sugar

Salt

Lime juice

Malaysian in origin, this sambal is a favorite of many ethnic groups in Sri Lanka. It is tucked away in Sri Lanka's famous lumpries, savory rice and curries wrapped snugly and baked in fresh banana leaves. You may also serve this sambal with rice and curries. Serve in small bowls, and it will give any casual meal a boost.

Directions

Add dried shrimp to a small frying pan over medium heat. When shrimp are partially roasted, add coconut and red chilies. Using a wooden spoon, stir shrimp, coconut, and chilies until coconut turns dark brown. Remove from heat.

In a small blender, combine roasted ingredients, shallots, ginger, garlic, coconut milk, and sugar with salt and lime juice to taste and blend to a smooth paste. Transfer to a small dish. When cool enough to handle, pat mixture into the shape of a hamburger patty. Serve at room temperature.

Yield: ½ cup (125 ml)

Green Chili and Coconut Sambal

This hot sambal is very common in Sri Lanka and India and is made on a grinding stone. You may use a mortar and pestle or a small blender instead. This very hot and pungent sambal is made in small quantities. It can accompany many dishes, from simple rice and curry to fancy buriyani preparations. My favorite way to enjoy this sambal is to coat fresh fish with it, smother the fish in olive oil, and bake wrapped in banana leaves.

½ teaspoon (2.5 ml) freshly ground black peppercorns

½ cup (125 ml) grated fresh coconut

3 jalapeños, sliced

10 curry leaves

2 garlic cloves

¼ cup (60 ml) chopped shallots

Juice of 1 to 1½ limes

1 to 1½ teaspoons (5 to 7.5 ml) sea salt, or to taste

Directions

Place all ingredients in a grinder and grind to a fairly smooth texture. Taste and season with more lime juice and salt if needed. Transfer to a small dish and serve.

Yield: ½ cup (125 ml)

Hot Chili Sambal

This sambal provides a spicy flavor contrast when served with a meal. It is a common accompaniment to breakfast breads and steamed flour preparations such as roti, milk rice, and simple rice and curry dishes. Hot chili sambal with butter is a favorite among Sri Lankans. I particularly enjoy mixing sambal with a spoonful of cream cheese and heaping it on crackers or crusty bread.

20 whole dried red chilies, stems removed

2 tablespoons (30 ml) Maldive fish

½ cup (125 ml) chopped shallots or onion

Lime or lemon juice

Salt

Directions

Place chilies, Maldive fish, and shallots in a blender with lime juice and salt to taste and blend to a medium-coarse paste. Transfer to a small dish and serve at room temperature. Keeps well refrigerated for 2 to 3 days.

Yield: ¾ cup (180 ml)

Deviled Potatoes

1 pound (453 g) medium baking potatoes, unpeeled and washed

2 tablespoons (30 ml) olive oil

1 cup (250 ml) sliced onion

1 tablespoon (15 ml) thinly sliced garlic

2 tablespoon (30 ml) crushed red pepper

1 teaspoon (5 ml) paprika

¼ teaspoon (1.25 ml) turmeric

1 teaspoon (5 ml) ground coriander

1 teaspoon (5 ml) ground cumin

4-inch (10 cm) piece of cinnamon stick

4 whole sprigs of curry leaves (optional)

4-inch (10 cm) piece of pandanus leaf (optional)

Salt

2 tablespoons (30 ml) unsalted butter, melted

Deviled potatoes are a favorite of both young adults and grownups in Sri Lanka. This spicy dish makes a delightful accompaniment not only to our favorite rice and curry meals but also to roast meat and chicken and sautéed seafood. Many enjoy a plain salad with a serving of this devilish yet delicious dish on the side. As the name implies, deviled potatoes are hot! A vegetarian favorite.

Directions

Cut potatoes lengthwise into even-size wedges and then into large dice. Place in a pot, add cold water to cover, and cook over medium heat until potatoes are barely cooked through, about 15 to 20 minutes. Drain potatoes in a colander and set aside to cool.

Preheat oven to 375°F (190°C).

In a large sauté pan, heat olive oil over medium heat. Add onions and cook until wilted. Stir in garlic, spices, curry leaves, and pandanus leaf and cook for 2 minutes. Remove from heat and fold in the potatoes with salt to taste.

Transfer to a baking pan, drizzle with butter, and roast uncovered for 35 to 40 minutes, turning often with a spatula to make sure potatoes brown evenly. Serve hot.

6 to 8 servings

Carrot Sambal

Carrot sambal comes in handy as a salad enhancer. Add a heaping spoonful to a salad of greens and walnuts dressed with a simple vinaigrette.

Directions

In a bowl, combine carrots, lemon juice, and black pepper and season with salt to taste.

Heat oil in a small sauté pan over medium heat and sauté onion, green chilies, and curry leaves until onions are wilted. Stir in carom and mustard seeds and cook a few seconds, until the seeds start to splutter. Add crushed red pepper and immediately remove pan from heat. Pour the contents of the pan on the carrots and toss to combine flavors. Refrigerate for 20 minutes. Serve at room temperature.

6 to 8 servings

¾ pound (340 g) carrots, trimmed, washed, peeled, and roughly grated

Juice of 1 lemon

½ teaspoon (2.5 ml) black pepper

Salt

1 tablespoon (15 ml) vegetable oil

1 small onion, chopped

4 green chilies with stems removed, sliced

8 curry leaves

½ teaspoon (2.5 ml) carom seeds

½ teaspoon (2.5 ml) black mustard seeds

1 teaspoon (5 ml) crushed red pepper

Parsley Sambal

1 bunch of parsley, washed

1 small onion, roughly chopped

4 green chilies with stems removed, roughly chopped

1 teaspoon (5 ml) black pepper

1 teaspoon (5 ml) crushed red pepper

Juice of 1 to 1½ lemons

Salt

½ cup (125 ml) grated fresh coconut

This beloved Sri Lankan recipe can be made with substitutes such as kale. Chopping the parsley in a food processor brings out an intense fresh parsley taste. Do include the stems; they add body to the sambal.

Directions

Wash parsley, then dry with paper towels.

In a food processor, combine parsley, onion, green chili, black pepper, and crushed red pepper and chop very fine. Transfer to a medium bowl and season mixture with lemon juice and salt to taste. Add coconut and mix well to combine flavors. Refrigerate for 20 minutes. Serve chilled.

8 servings

Pennywort "Gotukola" Sambal

This sambal is not only delicious but also packed with nutrients. Pennywort is slightly bitter, close in taste to watercress, and a good accompaniment to seafood. I love it by itself and enjoy a generous portion as a salad. Use the stems, which add crunch and body to the sambal. Make sure to wash the greens in several changes of water before use.

Directions

Shred pennywort greens fine. (You'll need about 1½ cups [375 ml].) Place in a bowl and add shallots, green and red chilies, coconut, and black pepper, then season with lime juice and salt to taste. Mix thoroughly to combine greens with seasonings. Serve at once.

5 servings

1 bunch pennywort (about 8 ounces [250 g]), including stems, washed and trimmed

½ cup (125 ml) thinly sliced shallots

2 green chilies, seeded and thinly sliced

2 red chilies, seeded and thinly sliced

½ cup (125 ml) grated fresh coconut

1 teaspoon (5 ml) black pepper

Juice of 1 large lime or lemon

Salt

"Kuni" Sambal

There are different kinds of dried shrimp. The word "kuni" refers to tiny shrimp available dried and sold in neat packages in Chinese and Japanese stores. They are usually clean, but I always wash them three times in cold water before using them. Keep in mind that some shrimp are salty. Serve this sambal with rice and curry.

Directions

Wash dried shrimp in cold water, drain well, and set aside.

Heat oil in a medium sauté pan over medium heat and cook onions and curry leaves until onions are wilted. Add remaining ingredients and season with lime juice and salt to taste. Cover pan and cook for about 5 minutes. Remove cover and cook 8 minutes more on medium heat, stirring constantly. Serve hot with rice and curry.

6 servings

1 cup (250 ml) dried shrimp ("kuni")

1 tablespoon (15 ml) vegetable oil

½ cup (125 ml) thinly sliced onion

8 curry leaves

1 fresh green chili

1 fresh red chili

2 teaspoons (10 ml) crushed red pepper

½ teaspoon (2.5 ml) paprika

1 tablespoon (15 ml) lime juice

Salt

"Serundeng"

1 teaspoon (5 ml) vegetable oil

1 cup (250 ml) coconut flakes

¼ cup (60 ml) onion flakes

$1/8$ cup (30 ml) garlic flakes

1 teaspoon (5 ml) dried ginger powder

1 teaspoon (5 ml) ground coriander

1 teaspoon (5 ml) ground cumin

1 teaspoon (5 ml) black pepper

1 teaspoon (5 ml) salt

2 tablespoons (30 ml) lime juice

1 cup (250 ml) unsalted roasted peanuts

This enticing Indonesian favorite, with coconut and peanuts as main ingredients, is usually served as an accompaniment to a rice and curry meal. But there are no limits to the uses of this exotic spicy condiment. I serve it as an appetizer in little dishes, accompanied by tiny spoons along with a bowl of cut fruit.

Directions

Place a medium skillet over medium heat. When the skillet is very hot, add oil and use paper towels to brush skillet with oil. Be careful not to burn your fingers.

Turn heat to low, add coconut, and stir continuously with a wooden spoon until coconut is a golden color. Add onion flakes and garlic flakes and stir until they are toasty and well blended with the coconut. Stir in ginger and spices with salt to taste and cook for a few minutes. Fold in lime juice and remove from heat. Allow mixture to cool completely before folding in peanuts. Store in an airtight jar and use within 1 week.

Yield: 2 cups (500 ml)

"Seeni" Sambal

½ cup (125 ml) vegetable oil

2 4-inch (10 cm) stems of lemongrass

15 curry leaves (optional)

1-inch (2.5 cm) piece of pandanus leaf

5 onions, thinly sliced

¼ cup (60 ml) minced ginger

¼ cup (60 ml) minced garlic

½ cup (125 ml) coarsely ground Maldive fish or ground dried shrimp

1 teaspoon (5 ml) cardamom pods

1 teaspoon (5 ml) ground cloves

4-inch (10 cm) piece of cinnamon stick

2 teaspoons (10 ml) cayenne pepper

1 teaspoon (5 ml) paprika

¼ cup (60 ml) tamarind pulp

2 tablespoons (30 ml) brown sugar

Salt

Many refer to this sambal as one of Sri Lanka's national condiments. This traditional sambal is a must for festive occasions and for a sumptuous Sunday afternoon family lunch of rich buriyani and curried meat, poultry, or fish. It is meant to be sweet and aromatic, spicy and hot, an ethereal combination, hence the name "seeni sambal," meaning "sweet sambal." Lemongrass, curry leaves, and pandanus leaf provide a unique aroma, and cardamom pods, cloves, and cinnamon give the exotic taste of spices. This sambal has good keeping qualities. Stored in a sterilized jar and refrigerated, it will last for a week or so.

Directions

Heat oil in a large sauté pan. Add lemongrass, curry leaves, and pandanus leaf and cook for 5 minutes. Add onions and cook on medium-high heat, stirring often, until onions are soft, translucent, and a light golden color. Add ginger, garlic, Maldive fish or dried shrimp, and spices and continue cooking over low heat for about 30 minutes. Stir often to prevent burning. Stir in tamarind pulp and sugar and season with salt to taste. Continue cooking over low heat for 25 more minutes, stirring often.

Remove from heat, take out and discard lemongrass and pandanus leaf, and cool. Transfer to a medium dish, picking out cardamom pods and cloves if you prefer. Serve at room temperature.

10 to 12 servings

Spicy "Chutney" Powder

This preparation is called "'chutney' powder," but it is an extremely hot sambal, an Indian favorite that is sprinkled on food, especially rice and curry.

Although this is a simple dish, it is prudent to read through the recipe and organize your ingredients and utensils before starting to cook. The main ingredients are deep-fried individually and will need to be placed on absorbent paper to remove any oil. Sesame seeds are the last ingredient that needs frying. They are so tiny that they cook quickly and can turn dark. You can prevent this by having a wooden board nearby where you can set down the hot frying pan and placing a small strainer securely over a small bowl for draining the oil from the fried sesame seeds.

½ cup (125 ml) vegetable oil

½ cup (125 ml), packed, whole dried red chilies, stems removed

¼ cup (60 ml) urad dal

¼ cup (60 ml) chana dal

2 tablespoons (30 ml) white sesame seeds

Sea salt

Directions

Heat oil in a medium sauté pan or skillet over low heat. Add chilies and fry until they turn crisp and dark red but are not burnt. Place chilies on paper towels to absorb excess oil.

Add urad dal to the pan and fry until it is crisp and turns a light golden brown. Transfer to a plate lined with paper towels.

Repeat process with chana dal.

Turn off heat and move the pan with hot oil to a wooden board in your work area. Add sesame seeds to the oil and immediately pour oil and sesame seeds into a strainer with a bowl underneath. When the oil has finished draining into the bowl, carefully turn the strainer over onto paper towels and deposit sesame seeds onto the paper.

Use paper towels to blot fried items and remove as much oil as possible. When cool, place chilies, dals, and sesame seeds in a bowl and season with salt to taste. Grind to a fine powder in a spice grinder and store in an airtight jar. When ready to serve, scoop out a small amount with a dry spoon and place in a small bowl. Provide a teaspoon to serve. Use within 1 to 2 weeks.

Yield: 1 cup (250 ml)

Easy Flavor Sprinkler

½ cup (125 ml) white sesame seeds

¼ cup (60 ml) roasted cumin seeds, coarsely crushed

1 tablespoon (15 ml) black pepper

1 tablespoon (15 ml) medium-fine sea salt

Use this mix to add flavor to a plate of rice and curry, a bowl of soup, plain steamed vegetables, or fish.

Directions

In a small skillet, lightly roast sesame seeds, then crush seeds coarsely in a spice grinder.

Transfer to a clean, dry container and fold in remaining ingredients. Cover container with a tight-fitting lid and store in a dry place. Use within 1 week.

Yield: 1 cup (250 ml)

Curry Leaf Sambal

30 sprigs of curry leaves, washed

1 tablespoon (15 ml) water

1 tablespoon (15 ml) thinly sliced shallots

1 green chili, thinly sliced

1 teaspoon (5 ml) minced garlic

1 teaspoon (5 ml) minced ginger

½ cup (125 ml) grated fresh coconut

1 teaspoon (5 ml) sugar

1 teaspoon (5 ml) black pepper

1 tablespoon (15 ml) lemon juice

Salt

This is a common sambal in Sri Lanka and India, where curry leaf plants grow in many backyards. The plant also grows profusely in Hawai'i, and the leaves are available in big cities around the world. Ranjit introduced the curry leaf plant to Hawai'i about forty years ago, and I recall seeing it featured in *Gourmet* magazine about thirty years ago! Serve this sambal with rice and curry, or be inventive and pair it with seafood.

Directions

Pull curry leaves off stems and discard stems. You'll need about 1 cup (250 ml) of curry leaves. In a blender, grind curry leaves with water to a smooth paste.

Transfer to a container, add shallots, green chili, garlic, ginger, coconut, sugar, black pepper, and lemon juice, and season with salt to taste. Mix and mash thoroughly to combine flavors. Place in a small dish and serve at room temperature.

6 servings

Lime Pickle Sambal

Lime pickle sambal is hot, tart, and salty. It is meant to be used in very small quantities and is so pungent that it will awaken jaded appetites! It is good with rice and curry or Indian breads. The main ingredient is a pickled lime. Making the pickles is very time-consuming, but with pickles on hand, it is easy to whip up little relishes such as this in no time. Otherwise, buy bottled pickled limes or lemons to make this sambal.

Directions

Cut the pickled lime into very fine strips and place in a bowl. Add shallots, green chilies, Maldive fish (if using), apple cider vinegar, and cold water. Set aside.

Brush a small sauté pan with vegetable oil and place over medium heat. Add red chilies to the hot pan and roast for about 4 minutes. Grind roasted chilies in a spice grinder and add to the seasoned lime pickles in the bowl. Mix well to combine flavors and transfer to a small serving dish.

Yield: 1 cup (250 ml)

1 pickled lime (see **Hot and Spicy Lime Pickles**, p. 101), seeded

6 shallots, thinly sliced

3 green chilies, thinly sliced

1 tablespoon (15 ml) Maldive fish (optional)

1 teaspoon (5 ml) apple cider vinegar

1 tablespoon (15 ml) cold water

1 teaspoon (5 ml) vegetable oil

6 dried red chilies, stems removed

Banana Blossom Sambal

1 banana flower (about 1½ pounds [680 g]), washed and stem trimmed

Salt

3 plum tomatoes, chopped

1 tablespoon (15 ml) crushed red pepper

1 tablespoon curry powder

1 tablespoon (15 ml) lemon juice

¼ cup (60 ml) vegetable oil

1 cup (250 ml) thinly sliced red onion

8 curry leaves

2 teaspoons (10 ml) chopped garlic

2-inch (5 cm) piece of cinnamon stick

1 teaspoon (5 ml) fenugreek seeds

6 crushed cardamom pods

¼ cup (60 ml) tamarind juice

¾ cup (180 ml) coconut milk

Banana flowers are beautiful, and sambals are delicious, but preparing the flowers for cooking is a tedious process. The sap in the flower stains and is difficult to wash away, so wear gloves when cutting the banana flower. Serve this delicious vegetable as you would any other vegetable!

Directions

Remove and discard coarse outer leaves of the banana flower. Place flower on a cutting board, hold by the stem end, and start slicing thinly, beginning at the tip of the flower. Keep turning the flower by the stem end as you slice, until you reach the end of the flower. Place sliced flower shreds in a bowl and sprinkle with 1 tablespoon (15 ml) of salt. Mix thoroughly, then let sit for about 1 hour.

Place brined flower shreds in a colander and wash away salt under cold running water. Squeeze water out of flower shreds a handful at a time, place in a container, and loosen the shreds. Add tomatoes, crushed red pepper, curry powder, and lemon juice. Mix and set aside.

Heat oil in a medium sauté pan over high heat and fry onions to a golden brown. Add curry leaves, garlic, cinnamon, fenugreek, and cardamom, turn heat to low, and fry for 4 to 5 minutes. Add seasoned flower shreds and stir to combine with seasonings. Mix in tamarind juice and coconut milk and add salt to taste. Continue cooking over low heat for 30 minutes, stirring often to prevent scorching. Serve hot or warm. Cover and refrigerate leftover sambal and reheat when needed. Keeps well for 1 week.

10 to 12 servings

Fried Eggplant and Cashew Sambal

In this recipe, the eggplant is fried in oil according to tradition, but you may toss sliced eggplant in a little olive oil and roast the slices in a hot oven if you prefer. Eggplant sambal is a standby for rice and curry and partners well with meat.

Directions

Trim the ends off eggplants and slice lengthwise into ¼-inch (0.6 cm) rounds. Sprinkle with 2 teaspoons (10 ml) salt and leave for 30 minutes. Wash eggplants and wipe dry with paper towels. Add turmeric and mix well to coat slices.

Heat oil in a small frying pan over medium heat. Fry cashew nuts until they turn a pale gold color, 30 to 40 seconds, then place on paper towels to drain.

Fry eggplant in batches. When slices are fried crisp and golden brown, place on paper towels to drain.

Remove all but 2 teaspoons (10 ml) of the oil in the frying pan and place pan over low heat. Add onion and green chilies and cook until onions are wilted. Stir in curry powder, black pepper, mustard, vinegar, sugar, and lemon juice and add salt to taste. Fold in fried eggplant and cashews to combine with seasonings and continue cooking over low heat for 1 to 2 minutes. Serve warm or at room temperature.

6 servings

1 pound (453 g) long eggplants

Salt

½ teaspoon (2.5 ml) turmeric

Oil for frying

1 cup (250 ml) cashew nuts

1 cup (250 ml) thinly sliced onions

2 green chilies, thinly sliced

2 teaspoons (10 ml) curry powder

1 teaspoon (5 ml) black pepper

1 tablespoon (15 ml) Dijon grainy mustard

1 tablespoon (15 ml) apple cider vinegar

1 tablespoon brown sugar

Juice of 1 lemon

Fried Bitter Melon Sambal

1 cup (250 ml) thinly sliced red onions

2 medium bitter melons, sliced very thin (about 2 cups [500 ml])

½ teaspoon (2.5 ml) turmeric

1 cup (250 ml) oil for frying

2 plum tomatoes (or your choice of tomatoes), thinly sliced

2 green chilies, sliced

1 teaspoon (5 ml) black pepper

1 teaspoon (5 ml) crushed red pepper

Juice of 1 lemon

Salt

¼ cup coconut milk

Fried bitter melon is not as bitter as the uncooked melon. Some of the bitterness is lost in the frying process.

Directions

Place sliced onions in a bowl and add enough cold water to cover. Refrigerate.

Place bitter melon slices in a bowl, add turmeric, and toss. Heat oil in a frying pan over moderate heat and fry bitter melon in small batches. When bitter melon is crisp and turns a light golden color, remove with a slotted spoon and place on paper towels to drain.

Pour onion slices and soaking water through a strainer, then refresh onion by holding strainer under cold running water. Let drain, then shake the strainer to remove any water that remains. Dry onion slices with paper towels and place on a salad platter.

Add tomatoes, green chilies, black pepper, crushed red pepper, and lemon juice and season with salt to taste. Mix well, then fold in fried bitter melon and coconut milk and serve.

6 servings

Bitter Melon Sambal

Bitter melon lives up to its name. Many love it, and many hate it. Some love it without its bitterness, and there are many techniques for reducing the bitter taste. Sprinkle salt on sliced bitter melon, leave for 30 minutes, and squeeze out the bitter juices. Or pour hot water on the slices, let steep for 10 minutes, and squeeze out the juices. However, nothing will completely rid bitter melon of its bitterness. Bitterness is a big part of the vegetable, so it is better to use it as is and enjoy it. As for me, I love bitter melon, especially when it is curried with tomatoes or made into a sambal.

It is important to remember that this vegetable will not take too much salt because of its bitterness, but it loves lemon or lime juice. Use white bitter melons in this recipe because they are so attractive in sambal. Bitter melon is said to be good for people with diabetes.

Directions

Trim ends of bitter melons and slice very thin. Remove and discard seeds if any.

Place bitter melon slices in a dish, add shallots, green chilies, and black pepper and season with lemon juice and salt to taste. Mix by gently crushing and tossing at the same time. Fold in coconut milk and grated coconut. Marinate for 15 minutes. Serve with rice and curry.

6 to 8 servings

2 tender medium bitter melons

½ cup (125 ml) thinly sliced shallots

2 thinly sliced green chilies

1 teaspoon (5 ml) black pepper

Lemon juice

Salt

¼ cup (60 ml) thick coconut milk

½ cup (125 ml) fresh grated coconut

Leek and Tomato Sambal

1½ pounds (650 g) leeks, white and light green parts only

1 tablespoon (15 ml) vegetable oil

½ cup (125 ml) chopped onion

1 tablespoon (15 ml) chopped garlic

1 cup (250 ml) small-diced tomatoes

1 tablespoon (15 ml) crushed red pepper, or to taste

1 teaspoon (5 ml) black pepper

1 teaspoon (5 ml) curry powder

1 tablespoon (15 ml) brown sugar

1 tablespoon (15 m) tamarind juice

½ cup (125 ml) thick coconut milk

Salt

The leek, a member of the lily family, has a cylindrical white stalk with a slightly bulbous root end and many flat, dark green, long leaves. The tender pale green and white parts are sweeter and stronger in flavor than a scallion and can be baked, cooked into a mild curry, used as a side dish, or made into a soup. However, a spicy leek sambal is unique.

Directions

Cut off and discard about 2 inches (5 cm) at the root end and top end of each leek, leaving only the light green and white parts. Slice leek in half lengthwise and place halves in a large bowl of cold water. Repeat until all the leeks are soaking in the bowl, then wash in several changes of water to get rid of the sand and dirt clinging to them. Drain water, making sure it runs clear, and place leeks on paper towels to dry. Cut leek halves into ½-inch (1.25 cm) slices. (You'll need about 2 cups [500 ml].)

In a sauté pan, heat oil over medium heat and sauté onions until they are a light golden color. Add garlic and cook for 1 minute, then add leeks and cook for 4 to 5 minutes. Fold in tomatoes, crushed red pepper, black pepper, and curry powder. Turn heat to medium high, fold in sugar, tamarind juice, and coconut milk, and season with salt to taste. Turn heat to low and cook for 8 to 10 minutes until tomatoes are soft. Serve hot or at room temperature.

6 to 8 servings

Coconut "Mallun"

"Mallun" refers to a cooking technique in which finely shredded leafy green vegetables and fresh grated coconut or other vegetables are briefly cooked in a clay pot. This fast-cooking technique preserves most of the nutrients, especially in the leafy green vegetables. Everybody loves coconut, and this dish takes it to new heights. It is good with rice and vegetable curries, as a side dish with seafood and meat, with savory breakfast dishes, and as a spread for sandwiches.

Directions

In a sauté pan, heat butter over medium heat and sauté onions until golden brown. Stir in ginger, garlic, curry leaves (if using), spices, and dried shrimp (if using). Continue to cook, stirring, for 1 to 2 minutes. Add water and stir in coconut and tomato. Cook for 4 to 5 minutes, stirring constantly to prevent scorching. The mixture should be moist. Season with lemon juice and add salt to taste.

6 to 8 servings

1 tablespoon (15 ml) unsalted butter

1 tablespoon (15 ml) chopped onion

1 teaspoon (5 ml) minced ginger

2 teaspoons (10 ml) minced garlic

8 curry leaves (optional)

1 teaspoon (5 ml) ground cumin

1 teaspoon (5 ml) ground coriander

¼ teaspoon (1.25 ml) turmeric

½ teaspoon (2.5 ml) crushed red pepper

1 tablespoon (15 ml) coarsely ground dried shrimp (optional)

½ cup (125 ml) water

1½ cups (375 ml) grated fresh coconut

1 chopped plum tomato

1 tablespoon (15 ml) lemon juice

Salt

Honey Roasted Baby Carrots

This recipe works just as well with regular carrots. Halve the smaller carrots, cut larger carrots diagonally into slices 1 inch (2.5 cm) thick, and roast as directed.

Directions

Preheat oven to 400°F (204°C).

Place carrots in a bowl and add olive oil, thyme, carom seeds, balsamic vinegar, honey, crushed red pepper, and black pepper and season with salt to taste. Mix well, coating carrots with seasonings, and transfer to a baking pan.

Roast for 40 to 45 minutes, turning a few times, until carrots are cooked through and glazed. Serve warm or at room temperature.

8 to 10 servings

2 pounds (680 g) whole baby carrots, trimmed, peeled, and washed

2 tablespoons (30 ml) olive oil

4 sprigs of fresh thyme

¾ teaspoon (3.75 ml) carom seeds

1 tablespoon (15 ml) balsamic vinegar

2 tablespoons (30 ml) honey

1 tablespoon (15 ml) crushed red pepper

1 teaspoon (5 ml) black pepper

Salt

Curried Pineapple

1 medium pineapple, peeled, cored, and quartered

1 tablespoon (15 ml) vegetable oil

½ cup (125 ml) chopped onion

1 teaspoon (5 ml) fenugreek

10 curry leaves

2-inch (5 cm) piece of pandanus leaf (optional)

4-inch (10 cm) piece of lemongrass stem

1½ teaspoons (7.5 ml) Dijon grainy mustard

1-inch (2.5 cm) piece of cinnamon stick

2 teaspoons (10 ml) ground coriander

1 teaspoon (5 ml) ground cumin

2 teaspoons (10 ml) ground fennel seeds

1 teaspoon (5 ml) cayenne pepper

⅛ teaspoon (0.62 ml) turmeric

Salt

1 cup (250 ml) coconut milk

2 teaspoons (10 ml) sugar (optional)

Curried pineapple is a common dish in Sri Lanka and a favorite with vegetarians.

Directions

Cut pineapple into ½-inch (1.25 cm) cubes. (You'll need about 2 cups [500 ml].)

Heat oil in a medium pan over medium heat and cook onion until golden. Add fenugreek, curry leaves, pandanus leaf (if using), and lemongrass and cook for 2 to 3 minutes. Fold in pineapple, mustard, and spices and add salt to taste. Stir in coconut milk and sugar (if using), cover pan, and simmer over low heat for 25 minutes, stirring frequently.

8 to 10 servings

Curried Mangoes

1 pound (453 g) mature Hawaiian green mangoes, peeled

Salt

1 tablespoon (15 ml) apple cider vinegar

2 tablespoons (30 ml) brown sugar

1 tablespoon (15 ml) Dijon grainy mustard

2 tablespoons (30 ml) vegetable oil

1 cup (250 ml) sliced onion

2 teaspoons (10 ml) minced ginger

2 teaspoons (10 ml) minced garlic

8 curry leaves

4-inch (10 cm) piece of lemongrass stem

4-inch (10 cm) piece of cinnamon stick

1 tablespoon (15 ml) ground coriander

2 teaspoons (10 ml) ground cumin

1 teaspoon (5 ml) ground fennel

2 teaspoons (10 ml) cayenne pepper

½ teaspoon (2.5 ml) turmeric

1 cup (250 ml) coconut milk

Fruit curries are among the vegetarian curries said to have been served in the court of Sinhalese king Kashyapa I in Sigiriya, Sri Lanka, as far back as the fifth century. Mango curry has a refined, rich taste and flavor and is a favorite around the country. It is even better when made with luscious Hawaiian mangoes.

Directions

Slice mangoes, discard seeds, and cut flesh into long, thin slices about ½ inch (1.25 cm) thick. Sprinkle with 2 teaspoons (10 ml) salt and set aside for 1 hour. Rinse and drain mango slices and dry with absorbent paper. Place in a bowl, add vinegar, brown sugar, and mustard and refrigerate for 1 to 2 hours.

In a medium pan, heat oil over medium heat and sauté onion until light golden brown. Add ginger, garlic, curry leaves, lemongrass, and cinnamon and cook 4 to 5 minutes. Stir in seasoned mango slices and cook over very low heat for 4 to 5 minutes. Set aside.

In the meantime, combine ground coriander, ground cumin, and ground fennel in a small skillet. Place over medium heat and stir with a wooden spoon while roasting to a dark, coffee-brown color.

Add the roasted spices, cayenne pepper, and turmeric to the mangoes and stir well to coat with seasonings. Fold in coconut milk, cover pan, and simmer over low heat, stirring frequently, for 20 to 25 minutes. Taste and season with more brown sugar and salt if needed. Serve with rice and curry.

8 to 10 servings

Roasted Eggplant Sambal

Eggplant sambal is perfect with any lamb dish, be it a roast leg of lamb, lamb chops, or rack of lamb. It is also a favorite with rice and lamb curry. If you prefer not to fry the eggplant, roast it in a 400°F (200°C) oven instead.

Directions

With a sharp knife, make cuts on the eggplants 1 inch (2.5 cm) long and 1 inch deep. Brush eggplants with some of the oil and reserve the rest for later.

Roast eggplants on a charcoal grill. Make sure the peels are scorched and the eggplants are cooked and soft inside. Peel eggplants, chop into bite-size pieces, and transfer to a small bowl. Set aside.

Heat reserved oil in a medium sauté pan over medium heat. When oil is medium-hot, add onion and red and green chilies, stir, and cook until onions are soft. Add mustard seeds and cumin seeds, cook a few seconds, then immediately stir in eggplant. Remove from heat and fold in tamarind juice, tomatoes, and lemon juice. Add sugar and season with salt to taste. Fold in coconut milk.

Place on low heat and cook for 2 to 3 minutes. Turn off heat and allow contents to cool in the pan. Spoon into a small dish. Refrigerate and let marinate for 1 to 2 hours. Use within 1 or 2 days.

6 servings

2 large round purple eggplant (about 1 pound [453 g])

3 tablespoons (45 ml) vegetable oil

2 tablespoons (30 ml) chopped onion

2 tablespoons (30 ml) chopped green chili

2 tablespoons (30 ml) chopped fresh red chili

1 teaspoon (5 ml) crushed black mustard seeds

1 teaspoon (5 ml) crushed cumin seeds

¼ cup (60 ml) tamarind juice

½ cup (125 ml) chopped tomatoes

1 tablespoon (15 ml) lemon juice

2 teaspoons (10 ml) sugar

Salt

¼ cup (60 ml) thick coconut milk

APPLE AND LEMON MARMALADE

PRESERVED LEMON WHEELS

RED PEPPER AND TOMATO JELLY

TOMATO CONFIT

PRESERVED PEACHES

PAPAYA AND PINEAPPLE MARMALADE

SPICY WINTER MELON PRESERVE

PRESERVED SPICY ORANGES

GREEN APPLE, APRICOT, AND PECAN PRESERVE

CARROT MARMALADE

SPICY KUMQUAT PRESERVE

KUMQUAT PRESERVE

STEWED RHUBARB

RHUBARB AND GREEN APPLE PRESERVE

RED ONION MARMALADE

LEMON CURD

PINEAPPLE AND LIME PRESERVE

PEAR, ORANGE, AND DATE PRESERVE

WI APPLE PRESERVE

APRICOT DIP

BRANDIED CHERRIES

PRESERVES

Preserving is a technique, and its products are known as preserves. Preserving techniques in use today have been around in different forms from ancient times. Almost all edible material can be preserved. Foods such as fruit, nuts, flowers, and vegetables may be preserved in various ways. Generally, they are cooked in alcohol, vinegar, and sugar syrup, which add flavor and help preserve. Spices such as cinnamon, nutmeg, cardamom, cloves, mace, and black pepper contribute fragrance. Jams, jellies, and marmalades are among the most common preserves. In taste, preserves range from simply sweet, to sweet and sour, to sweet and spicy. They are served as accompaniments to pastries and breads; starters such as salads; main dishes such as roasted meat and poultry and braised, roasted, or grilled fish; and desserts. Trendy spicy preserves are offered in very small portions as appetizers and desserts. Use nonreactive equipment for preparing, serving, and storing preserves.

Apple and Lemon Marmalade

3 lemons, thinly sliced and seeded

4 cups (1 L) cold water

8 large green apples, peeled, cored, and thickly sliced

4 cups (1 L) sugar

1 tablespoon (15 ml) cracked black pepper

2-inch (5 cm) piece of cinnamon stick

This is a delicious topping for ice cream, scones, or crackers. Although it is sweet, it is a winner with roast lamb, chicken, and pork. Cracked black pepper adds only a hint of heat in the background, letting the lemony glazed apples stand on their own. Tart green apples are best in this recipe.

Directions

Cut lemon slices into 1-inch (2.5 cm) pieces and soak in water overnight.

The next day, transfer lemons and their water to a medium pan, turn heat to low, and cook for 20 minutes, until lemons are tender. Add apples, sugar, black pepper, and cinnamon stick and cook until mixture is thick and shiny, about 30 to 35 minutes. Pour into jars, cool, cover, and refrigerate.

Yield: 2 pints (1 L)

Preserved Lemon Wheels

These preserves have a lingering aroma and golden hue. They are good with cooked fish, chicken, or veal.

Directions

Place lemon slices in a bowl and add 2 cups (500 ml) of the water. Sprinkle with salt and set aside for 25 to 30 minutes.

In a pan, combine sugar, honey, cloves, cinnamon stick, cardamom pods, and the remaining 2 cups (500 ml) of water. Turn heat to low and simmer for 10 minutes, or until syrupy. Strain lemon slices, refresh with cold water, and add to the syrup. Simmer over low heat for 30 minutes, until lemon slices are glazed. Cool, transfer lemon slices and spiced syrup to a jar, cover, and refrigerate.

Yield: 1 pint (500 ml)

4 lemons, sliced ¼ inch (0.6 cm) thick

4 cups (1 L) water

1 tablespoon (15 ml) salt

1 cup (250 ml) sugar

½ cup (125 ml) honey

8 whole cloves

1-inch (2.5 cm) piece of cinnamon stick

4 cardamom pods, slightly crushed

Red Pepper and Tomato Jelly

Red pepper jelly is a favorite accompaniment to cold dishes. Sauces and dressings may also be enriched with this jelly. Fold pepper jelly into mayonnaise for a salad dressing or stir into whipped cream and use as a topping for seafood. This jelly may be mild if you prefer less heat. Just use fewer jalapeños and serranos.

Directions

In a food processor, puree tomatoes and peppers. Transfer to a medium pan and add onions, garlic, and lemon juice. Place pan over medium heat and bring contents to a simmer. Simmer for 10 minutes. Using a fine-mesh sieve and a bowl, strain mixture, letting juices drip into the bowl beneath.

Pour the collected juices into a pan and add wine and sugar with salt to taste. Stir, so sugar starts to dissolve, and place over medium heat. Cook, stirring constantly, for 4 to 5 minutes. When the mixture begins to jell, remove from heat. Cool, then transfer to sterilized jars and store.

Yield: 2 pints (1 L)

1½ pounds (680 g) beefsteak tomatoes, peeled and coarsely chopped

1 pound (453 g) mix of red peppers, such as bell peppers, jalapeños, and serranos, stems removed, seeded, and chopped

2 onions, coarsely chopped

2 garlic cloves, crushed

½ cup (125 ml) lemon juice, strained

¼ cup (60 ml) red port wine

4 cups (1 L) sugar

Salt

Tomato Confit

1½ cups (375 ml) olive oil

½ cup (125 ml) sugar

1-inch (2.5 cm) piece of cinnamon stick

1 bay leaf

1 sprig of thyme

2 garlic cloves, crushed

36 cherry tomatoes, peeled

Confit is a method of preserving meat, especially poultry. The meat is cooked in its own fat and stored in a pot, covered with the fat, and refrigerated. Any remaining fat may be used for cooking; with duck confit, for example, the leftover fat can be used for roasting potatoes. Vegetables are also prepared using this method. These tomatoes are stunning with grilled or steamed asparagus. They not only look good but also taste delicious.

Directions

Preheat oven to 200°F (93°C).

Combine oil, sugar, cinnamon, bay leaf, thyme, and garlic in a baking pan. Add tomatoes, making sure they are covered with oil. Cover pan and bake for 45 minutes.

Cool in the cooking oil, then spoon tomatoes into a dish. Pour oil through a strainer over the tomatoes, cover dish, and refrigerate. Discard herbs and spices in the strainer. Use tomatoes as needed. Refrigerated, the vegetable confit keeps well for 1 month or more.

Yield: 1 pint (500 ml)

Preserved Peaches

I like to preserve peeled peach halves. They make an awesome garnish for roast game birds and a good accompaniment to ice cream, too.

Directions

In a pan, bring 4 cups of water to a boil. Carefully drop peaches into boiling water and leave in the pan for 1 minute. Remove peaches and drop into ice water. After about 6 minutes, peel peaches. The skin should come off easily. Cut peaches in half and remove and reserve the pits.

Place 2 cups of water, sugar, cloves, and cinnamon stick in a pan and add reserved peach pits. Bring to a simmer over low heat and add peach halves. Simmer for 15 minutes on very low heat.

Spoon peaches into a sterilized jar. Strain the syrup and pour over peaches, then add brandy and cover jar. Cool and refrigerate. Use after 3 months.

Yield: 1 pint (500 ml)

6 ripe peaches

4 cups (1 L) boiling water

Ice water

2 cups (500 ml) water

1 cup (250 ml) sugar

6 whole cloves

1-inch (2.5 cm) piece of cinnamon stick

½ cup (125 ml) brandy

Papaya and Pineapple Marmalade

4 ripe papayas

1 small pineapple

1 tablespoon (15 ml) grated orange peel

1 tablespoon (15 ml) grated lemon peel

¼ cup (60 ml) orange juice

¼ cup (60 m) lemon juice

1 tablespoon (15 ml) grated ginger

1 teaspoon (5 ml) black peppercorns

Sugar

Papaya and pineapple are favorite fruits, not only in Hawai'i but the world over. When they are plentiful, they may be used to make this delicious marmalade. Use it with breakfast breads and pastries and as a topping for ice cream and desserts. The papayas should be just ripe and soft, not overripe, for this recipe. The black peppercorns in the marmalade give it a very attractive appearance.

Directions

Trim the stem end of each papaya, wash, cut off the skin, and slice lengthwise into quarters. With a teaspoon, scoop out and discard papaya seeds. Cut quarters into big chunks, then cut chunks into ⅛-inch (0.3 cm) slices. (You'll need 4 cups [1 L] sliced.)

Wash pineapple and trim off and discard the leaf and stem ends. Place pineapple upright and slice off the skin. Cut away the eyes and slice pineapple lengthwise into four wedges. Place a wedge flat on its side and cut off the core. Repeat with remaining pineapple wedges. Slice wedges crosswise into ⅛-inch-thick pieces. (You'll need 1 cup [250 ml] sliced.)

Place sliced fruit in a medium pan and add orange and lemon peels, orange and lemon juices, ginger, and black peppercorns. Place pan over low heat and simmer for about 30 minutes. Set aside until cool enough to handle, then weigh cooked fruit and return to the pan.

Weigh out sugar equal to the weight of the cooked fruit and add to the pan. Place pan over low heat and simmer mixture for 30 minutes, stirring gently and frequently to prevent scorching. Cool, transfer to jars, cover, and refrigerate.

Yield: 1½ pints (750 ml)

Spicy Winter Melon Preserve

3 pounds (1.36 kg) winter melon, peeled and seeded (2 pounds [907 g] trimmed)

2-inch (5 cm) piece of cinnamon stick

6 whole cloves

6 cardamom pods, crushed

2 cups (500 ml) sugar

2 cups (500 ml) water

½ cup (125 ml) vinegar

½ cup (125 ml) white wine

In this dish, winter melon is preserved in a spicy, tangy syrup. It is glazed and translucent and fragrant with spices. For special occasions, I garnish roasted poultry with this unusual yet elegant preserve. It never fails to thrill my guests.

Directions

Cut winter melon into logs. Prick with a fork all over and wrap in a tea towel. Roll and press on melon to squeeze out as much liquid as possible. Cut into 2-inch (5 cm) cubes.

Combine remaining ingredients in a heavy-bottomed pan and simmer over low heat for 15 minutes. Add cubed melon and continue cooking over low heat, stirring occasionally, for 40 minutes. Remove from heat, cover, and let sit overnight.

The next day, simmer for 40 minutes over low heat. Transfer to sterilized jars. Cover, cool, and refrigerate. Keeps well for 2 to 3 weeks.

Yield: 2 pints (1 L)

Preserved Spicy Oranges

Preserved spicy oranges are always good with duck, along with its traditional watercress garnish. They are also an excellent companion for leg of lamb, grilled chops, and rack of lamb with mint.

Directions

Cut each orange into 8 wedges. Place in a large bowl, add enough water to cover, and sprinkle wedges with salt. Let sit overnight.

The next day, drain oranges in a colander and rinse with cold water.

Combine sugar, water, vinegar, cloves, and cinnamon stick in a heavy-bottomed pan, place over low heat, and bring contents to a simmer. Add oranges and simmer for 1 hour. Remove from heat, cool, cover pan, and let sit in syrup overnight.

The next day, cook oranges in syrup over low heat for 1 hour, until oranges are glazed. Let cool, store in a glass container, and refrigerate. Keeps well for 2 to 3 weeks.

Yield: 1½ pints (750 ml)

4 oranges

4 tablespoons (60 ml) salt

1½ cups (375 ml) sugar

1½ cups (375 ml) water

½ cup (125 ml) apple cider vinegar

4 whole cloves

2-inch (5 cm) piece of cinnamon stick

Green Apple, Apricot, and Pecan Preserve

This combination of apples, apricots, and pecans is crunchy, sweet, sour, and mildly spiced. This preserve is more like a chutney and makes a good substitute for jam at breakfast. I love to spread it lavishly on hot, buttered scones.

Directions

Combine apples, apricots, and pecans and set aside.

Place cumin, allspice, nutmeg, pepper, cinnamon stick, sugar, lemon juice, and vinegar in a medium pan and bring to a simmer over low heat. Add apples, apricots, pecans, and salt to taste and simmer 40 to 45 minutes or until thick and shiny. Remove and discard cinnamon stick. Cool and store in jars.

Yield: 1½ pints (750 ml)

5 large green cooking apples, peeled, cored, and diced medium

½ cup (125 ml) dried apricots, diced medium

¼ cup (60 ml) coarsely chopped pecans

¼ teaspoon (1.25 ml) ground cumin

¼ teaspoon (1.25 ml) ground allspice

¼ teaspoon (1.25 ml) grated nutmeg

½ teaspoon (2.5 ml) black pepper

1-inch (2.5 cm) piece of cinnamon stick

1 cup (250 ml) sugar

¼ cup (60 ml) lemon juice

¼ cup (60 ml) distilled vinegar

Salt

Carrot Marmalade

2 pounds (907 g) carrots, peeled and grated

2 bitter oranges, quartered, thinly sliced, and seeded

1 lemon, quartered, thinly sliced, and seeded

Sugar

1 teaspoon (5 ml) crushed fennel seeds

2 teaspoons (10 ml) crushed red pepper

Carrot marmalade is stunning and tastes as good as it looks. Its uses are limitless. Try adding it to a spinach or arugula salad or a frisée and walnut salad. It also works well as a condiment for couscous and cooked grains.

Directions

In a medium saucepan, combine grated carrots with just enough water to cover, add orange and lemon slices, and let sit overnight.

The next day, place pan over medium heat and cook until carrots are tender, about 25 to 30 minutes. When cool enough to handle, measure the carrot-citrus mixture, then transfer to a medium saucepan. For each cup (250 ml) of carrot-citrus mixture, add 2/3 cup (157 ml) of sugar. Add crushed fennel seeds and crushed red pepper and mix to combine. Cook over moderate heat for 40 minutes, or until mixture turns shiny. Cool and store.

Yield: 2 pints (1 L)

Spicy Kumquat Preserve

1 pound (453 g) kumquats

4 tablespoons (60 ml) salt

2 cups (500 ml) sugar

2 cups (500 ml) water

1 cup (250 ml) white vinegar

2-inch (5 cm) piece of cinnamon stick

4 whole cloves

4 cardamom pods

1 bay leaf

Use this kumquat preserve in sauces, as a garnish, and in compound butters. To use the kumquats, press out seeds and use whole or chop, dice, or cut into strips.

Directions

Place kumquats in a medium bowl, add water to cover, and sprinkle with salt. Let sit overnight.

The next day, drain kumquats in a colander and rinse with cold water. Prick with the tip of a knife.

Combine sugar, water, vinegar, cinnamon stick, cloves, cardamom pods, and bay leaf in a heavy-bottomed medium pan and bring to a simmer over low heat. Add kumquats and simmer for 30 minutes. Leave kumquats in syrup overnight.

The next day, put kumquats into a strainer held over the pan and drain syrup into the pan. Place drained kumquats in a bowl and set aside.

Place the pan of syrup over low heat and bring to a simmer. Add kumquats and simmer for 8 to 10 minutes. Cool, then transfer to jars. Refrigerate for 2 weeks before using. Keeps well for 2 to 3 weeks.

Yield: 1½ pints (750 ml)

Kumquat Preserve

Select large juicy kumquats for this recipe. The preserve, which is more like a jam, is lovely on hot scones and mini tarts. It is also a great accompaniment to a roast veal loin or veal chops. One of my favorite menus, reserved for family and friends, is composed of roast veal loin served with kumquat preserve and a pan sauce enriched with brandy, along with bitter greens sautéed in butter and roasted glazed butternut squash as sides.

1 pound (453 g) kumquats, washed

Sugar

Juice of 1 large lemon

2 teaspoons (10 ml) cracked black peppercorns

1 tablespoon (15 ml) brandy

Directions

Cut kumquats into 3 or 4 slices each. Remove and discard seeds. Place kumquats in a heavy-bottomed medium saucepot and add just enough water to cover. Cook over low heat until fruit is soft, about 35 minutes. Carefully measure cooked kumquats and return to the saucepot.

Measure out an amount of sugar equal to the amount of kumquats and add to the saucepot along with lemon juice and black peppercorns. Simmer over low heat for 30 minutes or so, stirring frequently, until contents are thick and glistening. Add brandy, cover saucepot, and remove from heat. Cool and store.

Yield: 1 pint (500 ml)

Stewed Rhubarb

This spicy stewed rhubarb is best as an ice cream topping or part of a fruit salad.

Directions

Remove outer stringy peel from rhubarb and slice ½ inch (1.25 cm) thick. (You'll need 1½ cups [375 ml]). Combine rhubarb and remaining ingredients in a pan and season with a pinch of salt to taste. Cook over low heat for about 40 minutes, until the mixture is the consistency of marmalade.

Yield: 1½ cups (375 ml)

4 to 5 rhubarb stems

1 tablespoon (15 ml) grated ginger

½ teaspoon (2.5 ml) cayenne pepper

1 teaspoon (5 ml) ground cloves

2-inch (5 cm) piece of cinnamon stick

1 cup 250 ml) sugar, or to taste

¼ cup (60 ml) lemon juice

¾ cup (180 ml) red port wine

Salt

Rhubarb and Green Apple Preserve

This preserve is delicious on toast or as a filling for pastry cups. My favorite ways to serve this spicy preserve is as an accompaniment to roast pork or roast lamb with roasted root vegetables and as a topping for coconut ice cream. Tart green apples such as Granny Smith are ideal for this recipe.

Directions

In a medium saucepan, heat butter over low heat and cook apples until they start to soften. Add rhubarb, wine, lemon juice, and ginger and simmer for 10 minutes. Add cinnamon, crushed red pepper, and sugar, using more or less according to taste. Season lightly with salt and mix gently to combine all ingredients. Cook over medium heat, stirring often, for 30 to 35 minutes, until the mixture is thick and shiny.

Cool and store. Once opened, the preserve will keep for 2 to 3 weeks.

Yield: 1½ pints (750 ml)

2 tablespoons (30 ml) unsalted butter

2 cups (500 ml) peeled, cored, and diced green apples

1 cup (250 ml) peeled, sliced rhubarb stems

½ cup (125 ml) white wine

½ cup (125 ml) lemon juice

1 tablespoon (15 ml) ground ginger

½ teaspoon (2.5 ml) ground cinnamon

½ teaspoon (2.5 ml) crushed red pepper

2 cups (500 ml) sugar, or to taste

Salt

Red Onion Marmalade

3 cups (750 ml) thin crosswise slices
of red onion

2 ounces (56 g) unsalted butter

2-inch (5 cm) piece of cinnamon stick

1 cup (250 ml) sugar, or to taste

1 cup (250 ml) red port wine

½ cup (125 ml) red wine vinegar

½ teaspoon (2.5 ml) cayenne pepper

Salt

Red onion marmalade is good with roast beef, especially when it is served with a red wine sauce. Creamed horseradish is also an essential accompaniment to roast beef and is generally available in grocery stores.

Directions

Loosen onion slices into rings. Heat butter in a large sauté pan and cook onions over high heat until soft. Add cinnamon stick, sugar, wine, vinegar, and cayenne pepper. Season lightly with salt to taste and cook for about 40 minutes, stirring often, until mixture has a jamlike consistency.

Yield: 2 cups (500 ml)

Lemon Curd

1 cup (250 ml) sugar

½ cup (125 ml) unsalted butter

Grated zest and juice of 2 large lemons

3 eggs, beaten and strained

Lemon curd is a lovely filling for tarts or mini tarts crowned with meringue. You may also serve it with sliced cake or scones.

Directions

Place sugar, butter, grated lemon zest, and lemon juice in a double boiler and stir until butter melts and sugar dissolves. Add eggs and continue stirring vigorously to prevent the mixture from curdling. When the curd is thick, after about 8 minutes, pour into a sterilized container, cool, and refrigerate.

Yield: 1½ cups (375 ml)

Pineapple and Lime Preserve

1 ripe medium pineapple, peeled, quartered, and cored

3 ripe limes, thinly sliced and seeded

2 cups (500 ml) water

4 makrut lime leaves, gently crushed

1 teaspoon (5 ml) black pepper

2 pounds (907 g) sugar, or to taste

I love this preserve with fine crackers and a soft cheese such as Brie or goat cheese. It is also a zesty accompaniment to baked ham.

Directions

Cut pineapple very thinly, almost into shreds. Place in a heavy-bottomed pan with lime slices, water, and makrut lime leaves. Simmer over low heat for about 45 minutes or so. Remove and discard makrut lime leaves. Add black pepper and sugar, using more or less according to taste. Continue cooking, stirring often, for about 10 minutes, until thick and shiny. Cool, transfer to a sterilized jar, cover, and store.

Yield: 1 pint (500 ml)

Pear, Orange, and Date Preserve

Serve this preserve with a cheese platter garnished with roasted nuts and crisp romaine lettuce.

Directions

Chop pears, oranges (including peel), and dates. Mix with chopped onion and set aside.

Place vinegar, orange juice, brown sugar, and ginger in a pan with salt to taste and bring to a simmer over medium heat. Add fruit-and-onion mixture and simmer on low heat for about 1 hour. Cool and store.

Yield: 1 pint (500 ml)

1 pound (453 g) pears, peeled and cored

2 oranges with peel, quartered and seeded

4 ounces (113 g) seedless dates

1 tablespoon (15 ml) chopped onion

1 cup (250 ml) apple cider vinegar

2 cups (500 ml) orange juice

¾ pound (340 g) brown sugar, or to taste

¼ cup (60 ml) minced ginger

Salt

Wi Apple Preserve

For preserves, wi apples are at their best when they are just turning yellow and are slightly soft. The fruit is delicious when preserved whole with seeds. Those who are familiar with it enjoy sucking on the preserved fruit and avoiding the seeds, which are prickly and can hurt the mouth.

Directions

Wash and peel wi apples. Use a fork and prick all over.

Put sugar, water, cinnamon stick, mace, and cardamom pods in a medium pan over low heat and bring to a simmer. Turn heat to medium, stir in fruit, and continue cooking, stirring often, for about 40 minutes, until syrup is thick and shiny and fruit is translucent. Fold in rose water. Cool and transfer to a sterilized jar, cover, and refrigerate.

Yield 1½ pints (750 ml)

12 to 15 half-ripe wi apples (about 1 pound)

2 cups (500 ml) sugar

1½ cups (375 ml) water

2-inch (5 cm) piece of cinnamon stick

½ blade of mace

6 cardamom pods

1 tablespoon (15 ml) rose water

Apricot Dip

½ cup (125 ml) dried apricots, diced small

1 tablespoon (15 ml) golden raisins

1 tablespoon (15 ml) balsamic vinegar

1 tablespoon (15 ml) apple cider vinegar

Juice of 1 orange

2 teaspoons (10 ml) sugar, or to taste

1 teaspoon (5 ml) black pepper

¼ teaspoon (1.25 ml) crushed red pepper

2 teaspoons (10 ml) sugar, or to taste

Salt

This dip is for roasted vegetables but could also serve as a sauce for roast lamb or roast game hen.

Directions

Place all ingredients in a small pan and add sugar and salt to taste. Simmer for 10 minutes over low heat. Cool. In a blender, blend to a coarse texture. Spoon into a small bowl and serve.

Yield: 1 cup (250 ml)

Brandied Cherries

1 pound (453 g) cherries, pitted and stems removed

½ cup (125 ml) sugar

3 cups (750 ml) brandy

For this recipe, the cherries should not be too ripe. After four months, the preserved cherries will have absorbed the alcohol and be full of flavor, and the alcohol, in turn, will be flavored by the cherries and become a fruity liqueur.

Directions

Place cherries and sugar in a sterilized jar. Pour in brandy and seal the jar. Shake the jar twice a day for 1 week. Set cherries aside for 4 months before using.

Yield: 1 pint (500 ml)

Spices give individuality and variety to foods. They are used whole, crushed, ground raw and cooked, roasted and ground, or fried in oil and ground (see, for example, **Spiced Yogurt,** p. 94, and **Banana Relish,** p. 38). It is important to understand the characteristics of individual spices so that they can be blended harmoniously with food. Spices have their individual aromas, and when certain spices are blended, crushed, or roasted and ground, they give a complex aroma to food.

Whole Spices

Whole spices—cinnamon sticks, black peppercorns, cloves, cumin seeds, star anise, and cardamom pods—are used to flavor stocks, sauces, and rice preparations. Whole spices used in stocks and sauces are easily removed by straining. In rice dishes, spices rise to the top of cooked rice and may be picked out with a pair of tongs and discarded before serving.

Infusing Spices

Steeping flavoring ingredients such as herbs or spices in a hot liquid infuses the liquid with their flavors. Infusing a minute quantity of saffron threads in a very small quantity of hot water or cream and adding both liquid and threads to dishes such as saffron rice contributes color, fragrance, and flavor to the rice. Peppercorn- and clove-infused cream or milk is strained and added to sauces and custards. Milk or sugar syrups infused with cinnamon, cardamom, or mace are used in desserts.

Grating Spices

Spices such as nutmeg need to be grated and are at their best when grated directly onto food. Use a hand grater or spice mill to grate these spices.

Crushing and Bruising Spices

Some recipes call for cracking or bruising spices such cardamom, peppercorns, and allspice. Many spices release more fragrance when slightly crushed. To crush or bruise them, place them in a polyethylene bag on a heavy surface and crush them with a rolling pin. You may also use a mortar and pestle for this purpose.

Grinding Raw Spices

An electric coffee grinder is excellent for grinding spices. Reserve coffee grinder exclusively for this purpose. Store ground spices in an airtight container and place in a cool, dry place. A small china mortar and pestle is handy for grinding small amounts of spices.

Roasting and Grinding Spices

Use a heavy cast iron skillet to dry-roast whole spices. You may use a sauté pan or frying pan to roast spices if a skillet is unavailable. Place the skillet over medium heat and add spices when the skillet is very hot. Be careful not to overcrowd the skillet. Stir spices with a wooden spoon and shake skillet occasionally. After about 2 minutes, the spices will begin to change color and the skillet will start to smoke. Keep stirring the spices for about 2 more minutes, until they turn a darker golden brown and smell fragrant as they release their essential oils. Remove from heat and set aside.

Spices should be crisp to the bite when tested. Transfer roasted spices to a clean bowl and grind in electric grinder before they cool down. As soon as the ground spices have cooled, place in an airtight container and store in a cool, dry place. Roasted ground spices may be sprinkled on curries, vegetables, fresh sliced fruit, fresh chutneys, and raita. (For roasted and ground spices, see **garam masala** in blended spices [p. 226] and **masala** in the glossary [p. 242].)

Frying Spices

It takes time to master the technique of frying spices in oil in order to perfume or add fragrance and flavor to food. Fried spices enrich vegetable curries, dal preparations, fresh chutneys, and raita.

Place a small frying pan over low heat, add a little oil, and turn heat to medium. When the oil is very hot, add the spices, stirring constantly, so that they will not burn. Most delicate spices will brown almost instantly. If you are frying seeds, such as mustard or cumin, it is important to have a light lid at hand so that you can hold it over the pan and prevent popping seeds from flying out of the pan and into your eyes. The seeds will start to pop and splutter when they are done. If you are frying a combination of spices, add the larger spices to the oil first and continue adding in order of decreasing size. Immediately remove the pan from heat and pour the fried spices onto the food you need to flavor.

One way of using asafetida is to add $1/8$ teaspoon to a pan in which you are frying black mustard seeds and fry for a few seconds before pouring the contents on food. The asafetida will perfume the oil with the enticing smell of onions. Curry leaves and asafetida are also fried together and are then added to vegetable and dal curries.

Blended Spices (masala)

Garam Masala

2 tablespoons (30 ml) cardamom seeds

2-inch (5 cm) piece of cinnamon stick

1 teaspoon (5 ml) black cumin seeds or cumin seeds

2 teaspoons (10 ml) whole cloves

1 tablespoon (15 ml) black peppercorns

⅓ of a whole nutmeg

A blend of aromatic spices that have been roasted, ground, and generally mixed with water or coconut milk to form a paste, garam masala is used in North and South Indian styles of cooking. It is added during the initial stages of cooking, although some recipes call for sprinkling it over food just before it is done or over the finished dish. There are many blends and recipes for garam masala, some hotter or more aromatic.

Directions

Place cardamom, cinnamon, black cumin seeds, cloves, and peppercorns in a small skillet and warm over low heat for 2 to 3 minutes. Transfer to a spice grinder and grind until smooth. Grate nutmeg and add to the mix. Store in an airtight container in a cool, dry place.

Yield: ¼ cup

Chaat Masala

Chaat masala is a blend of ground spices. It is tart and spicy and partners well with freshly sliced fruit, fruit salads, and fruity snacks. This masala is best made in small quantities, as its aroma evaporates quickly.

Directions

Heat a small skillet on medium heat. Add dried pomegranate seeds, black peppercorns, cumin seeds, and carom seeds. Stir with a wooden spoon over medium heat for 1 to 2 minutes or until ingredients are crisp and fragrant. Remove from the skillet and let cool.

Transfer roasted ingredients to an electric spice grinder and grind a few seconds. Add sea salt and grind contents to a fine powder. Transfer the ground mixture to a small bowl. Add mango powder, asafetida, cayenne pepper, and garam masala to the bowl and mix well using a wooden spoon.

Transfer the masala to a small jar, cover the jar, and keep it in a dry place. Use as needed. Generally, chaat masala is best soon after it is made.

Yield: approximately ½ cup

1 teaspoon (5 ml) sun-dried pomegranate seeds

1 teaspoon (5 ml) black peppercorns

1 teaspoon (5 ml) cumin seeds

1 teaspoon (5 ml) carom seeds

1 teaspoon (5 ml) sea salt

1 teaspoon (5 ml) mango powder

1 teaspoon (5 ml) asafetida

1 teaspoon (5 ml) cayenne pepper

1 teaspoon (5 ml) garam masala

acidulated water. Water mixed with a small amount of lemon juice or vinegar. Soaking prepared fruits and vegetables in acidulated water for a short time before use will prevent discoloration.

allspice (*Pimenta dioica*). The allspice berry has an all-in-one aroma of mixed spices such as nutmeg, mace, cloves and cinnamon. Allspice berries are pungent and strong and look like large peppercorns with rough brown skins. They are used ground or whole and also in pepper blends, where they contribute a pleasing aroma.

apple cider vinegar. See **vinegar**

asafetida (*Ferula asafetida*). Asafetida is available in both lump and powdered forms, smooth or gritty. Asafetida lumps are usually brown in color and odorless and can be ground as needed. The ground form is an attractive creamy yellow color and releases a pungent smell that some may find repulsive. Cooking transforms its strong odor to a pleasing aroma.

Asafetida is an antidote for flatulence and is widely used in India and the northern part of Sri Lanka. The spice is a welcome addition to vegetarian dishes, many of which are based on pulses. It also flavors pickles and relishes. Asafetida is used in minute amounts and is best purchased in very small quantities. Buy the ground spice in containers or choose a lump of asafetida and grind as needed.

balsamic vinegar. See **vinegar**

basil (*Ocimum* spp.). Basil is a common herb used in cooking. There are many varieties of basil, but the common sweet basil is the most widely used. The soft, light green leaves have a sweet aroma, a strong crushed-clove flavor, and a peppery taste. It has an affinity for tomatoes, garlic, and olive oil and is used extensively in

Mediterranean cuisines, such as in pesto sauce, fresh relishes, and salads with tomatoes and cheese. Thai basil is an essential in Thai cuisine. Dried basil is available but is not a suitable ingredient for cooking because it lacks fragrance.

basmati. Generic name for a variety of long-grain rice grown along the foothills of the Himalayas in northern India. This rice has a unique aroma when cooked. Some consider it the best rice in the world.

bay leaf (*Laurus nobilis*). The dried leaves of the European laurel are used in many ways. They add flavor to vegetables, rice dishes, soups, sauces such as béchamel, tomato sauce, pickling mixes, and marinades and in baking and braising meat and poultry. Bay leaves are tough even after being cooked for a long time, so it is added at the beginning of cooking and removed when it has imparted sufficient flavor.

bitter melon (*Momordica charantia*). Bitter melon is also known as bitter gourd, and true to its name, it is very bitter. This warty-skinned gourd is mostly pale green in color. It is best used when young, when the whole gourd, including seeds and pith, are edible. Its medicinal uses are well known across Asia.

black cumin (*Cuminum nigrum*). Black cumin is sweeter in aroma and has a more refined taste than regular cumin. Black cumin seeds resemble caraway seeds but are smaller. They are usually used whole and lightly roasted in lamb dishes and rich rice pilafs. Black cumin is a rare variety of cumin and is available in Indian stores. Regular cumin may be substituted for black cumin.

black mustard seeds (*Brassica nigra*). The hottest and most popular of the mustard seeds, black mustard seeds are slightly larger than poppy seeds and purplish-brown in color. They are referred to as black because they are closer to black than brown in color. Black mustard seeds are popular in Sri Lankan and Indian cooking and are used crushed or whole and fried in oil, ground, crushed, or powdered.

black pepper (*Piper nigrum*). Black pepper has an earthy flavor and is very rich and pungent. It is a versatile spice, one of the oldest and most popular spices in the world. It enhances other flavors and is often used in curry powders and garam masala (see **masala**). Unlike most spices, black pepper is used not only in cooking but also as a table condiment.

black peppercorns. See **peppercorns**

black rice. Black rice is cultivated mainly in Southeast Asia. There are many varieties of black rice. Some are glutinous, and in Asia, this rice is mainly cooked with coconut milk and served with choice fruits as dessert. Black rice is sold online and in health food stores, which carry a variety of black rice, among them one from China known as "forbidden rice." Legend has it this ancient grain was referred to as "longevity rice" and was reserved for the emperors of China. This rice has an appealing, deep purplish-black color, a soft texture, and a roasted nutty flavor.

blanching. Blanching is part of a combination cooking method in which food is partially or briefly cooked in boiling water or fat. This method is used to remove undesirable flavors, to prepare food for freezing, and to loosen the peels of tomatoes and fruits such as peaches.

bouquet garni. Bouquet garni is used to introduce flavorings to stocks, soups, and sauces. A standard bouquet garni is a bunch of herbs consisting of parsley stems, tarragon, thyme, bay leaf, leeks, and celery tied into a bundle with kitchen string. The bouquet garni is removed after flavors have been extracted. Quantities of ingredients for bouquet garni should be determined by the amount of liquid it is used to flavor. See also **sachet.**

brown mustard seeds (*Brassica juncea*). Brown mustard seeds range in color from light to dark brown and are not as hot and pungent as black mustard seeds. They are an inexpensive substitute for black mustard seeds, which are not easily available and costly because they are harvested by hand.

buriyani. A rich rice preparation layered with savory lamb, chicken, or beef; fragrant with saffron, spices, and herbs; and enriched with fruits, nuts, and ghee or butter. Buriyani is the central dish for special dinners and is served with several chutneys, pickles, and savory breads.

capers (*Capparis rupestris*). Capers are the unopened flower buds of caper bushes, cured in wine vinegar brine, olive oil, or plain salt. The cured buds take on a sharp, salty, sour flavor and are used with seafood. It is an indispensable ingredient in tartar sauce. The small capers from the Provence region in France are known as nonpareils, meaning "without equal."

cardamom (*Elettaria cardamomum*). Cardamom pods, or whole cardamoms, contain small black seeds with a memorably intense, sweet, lemony fragrance. There are two varieties of cardamom, green and black. Green cardamom, the better of the two, is natural and unbleached and is available whole or ground. Black cardamom is a little larger, with a thicker skin. Whole black cardamom is used in North Indian rice pilaf, meat and poultry dishes, and spice mixes. Black cardamom is an essential spice in savory and sweet dishes around the world.

carom (*Carum copticum*). Carom (also known as ajwain) is the seed of a plant that is native to southern India and is also grown in the Middle East. Carom are small, striped, greenish-brown seeds that resemble celery and cumin seeds but are much smaller in size. They are available whole. When slightly bruised, they release a distinctive, strong thymelike aroma yet are much stronger in flavor than thyme. Crush them between your fingertips before use, to release the aroma. The seeds are used in vegetable and fish preparations, pastries, and breads.

carryover cooking. This is cooking that occurs after food is removed from a heat source, due to the residual heat in the food.

cayenne pepper. See **chilies**

chaat masala. See **masala**

chana dal. Chana dal is a lentil. It is very much like yellow split peas but a little smaller. Yellow split peas are a good substitute for chana dal. When roasted or fried and ground, it functions as a spice. It is also used in soups and stews.

chapati. This bread is made daily in many Indian and Sri Lankan homes. Whole wheat flour and water are kneaded and rolled by hand into thin rounds, then baked on a hot griddle.

chervil (*Anthriscus cerefolium*). Chervil (also known as sweet cicely) is a member of the parsley family. It resembles parsley, with lacy, feathery leaves and a delicate, sweet anise flavor. Fresh chervil is fragile and becomes colorless and loses its flavor when subjected to heat. It is best used as a garnish. Chervil is also available in chopped dried form and may be used in soups, fish, poultry, and egg dishes.

chili paste. Many varieties of chili paste are available in Asian grocery stores. The most popular chili paste is *sambal oelek,* a spicy, ground red chili paste that is a favorite among Asians.

chili sauce. A favorite condiment made with tomatoes, hot chilies, onions, vinegar, sugar, and spices. It has the consistency of ketchup.

chilies (*Capsicum annus*). Chilies are commonly used to impart spicy heat to food. They are the fruits of a large variety of plants in the Capsicum family. Their characteristic pungency comes from capsaicin. Fresh chilies come in a range of colors—from yellow, to orange, to green, to purple—and shapes, including tiny, thin, long and tapering, plump, large, bulbous, and crinkly. Levels of heat and flavor vary, too, from mild and sweet to fiery. Some red chilies are dried, a process that darkens their color.

Cuisines around the world make extensive use of chilies. Curries from India, Sri Lanka, and Thailand depend on chilies for their characteristic heat, as do Indonesian and Malaysian sambals. South America, Africa, Mexico, and the American South depend on chilies to kick up the spicy heat in their specialties.

There are many chili products. **Cayenne pepper** is a very finely ground powder from a particular variety of hot chili. **Dried red chilies** are available whole, some with stems still attached, and hot red chilies are sold in the form of **crushed red pepper.** Fresh red or green chilies are available pickled or brined. **Hawaiian chilies**, also known as bird's eye chilies, are red or yellow, about an inch (2.5 cm) long, and extremely hot. They are used to make the famous **Hawaiian Chili Pepper Water** (p. 29).

chives. French chives (*Allium schoenprasum*) are an herb in the onion family, with bright green, slender, hollow leaves and purple or pink flowers. They have a mild, sweet onion flavor and are used with eggs, potatoes, fish, and shellfish. They are an excellent garnish for soups and sauces and enhance relishes and salads.

Flat-leaf chives (*Allium tuberosum*), or garlic chives, are much stronger in flavor. When using chives, it is best to snip them with kitchen shears or cut them with a sharp knife, in order to avoid crushing them. Chives make an attractive garnish.

cilantro. See **coriander**

cinnamon (*Cinnamomum zelanicum*). Native to Sri Lanka, the spice is made from the inner bark of the evergreen tree. **Cinnamon sticks** or quills are made by layering paper-thin strips of cinnamon bark and rolling them up, then treating and drying the sticks. The orange-brown sticks have a sweet, distinct flavor and an exotic fragrance and are referred to as "Ceylon cinnamon" or "true cinnamon." It is a popular spice the world over. The bark of the Cassia species is also sold as cinnamon and is known as "false cinnamon." Ceylon cinnamon is brittle, whereas false cinnamon is woody and tough due to the presence of the outer bark. Cinnamon is available ground or in sticks.

cloves (*Syzigium aromaticum*). Cloves are the dried unopened flower buds of the tropical evergreen tree. When dried, the buds turn a red-brown color. Cloves are aromatic, pungent, and slightly astringent. They are available whole or ground and are used in both forms as a flavoring in meat preparations, pilaf, stocks, and sauces. When using whole cloves in rice pilaf, it is best to discard the cloves, which are too hard to chew. Clove oil is distilled from parts of the clove tree and has antiseptic and preservative qualities

coconut (*Cocos nucifera*). Coconut is the fruit of the coconut palm. **Coconut chips, coconut flakes, grated coconut,** and **shredded coconut** are made from the dried flesh of the coconut and are available sweetened or unsweetened. **Grated fresh coconut** is available packaged in fresh or frozen form. Dried shredded coconut, also known as desiccated coconut, is available sweetened or unsweetened and is used mainly in bakeries.

Coconut milk is the milky liquid extracted from the grated flesh of mature coconuts. It is a mistake to refer to the clear liquid inside the coconut as "coconut milk." The liquid inside a coconut is coconut water. Coconut oil is obtained from the dried coconut flesh known as copra.

coconut vinegar. See **vinegar**

condiments. Some condiments are prepared, such as mustards and creamed horseradish. Brined capers, pickled gherkins, bottled pickles and relishes, and sauces such as ketchup, chili sauce, and soy sauce are all widely available. These condiments are added while cooking to enhance the flavors of certain foods. Some, known as table condiments, are added to food at the table.

coriander (*Coriandrum sativum*). The seeds and leafy parts of the coriander plant have very different flavors and cannot be used as substitutes for each other. The leafy parts are also known as cilantro and Chinese parsley. Cilantro is widely used in Asian and Mexican cuisines, in relishes and salads, and as a garnish in stir-fries. It has a strong, sharp, citrus flavor that is pleasing to many but unpleasant to some.

Coriander seeds are a little larger than peppercorns and creamy brown in color. They have an orangelike sweet taste and a pleasing aroma. They are used whole or crushed in stocks and with other pickling spices or ground in roasted or raw spice blends. **Ground coriander** may also be used alone in vegetarian curries. It is an important spice in Indian, Sri Lankan, and Mediterranean cooking and is also known for its medicinal and antibacterial qualities.

crushed red pepper. See **chilies**

cumin (*Cuminum cyminum*). The small, oval, ridged seeds from the cumin plant are the source of this spice. The seeds are creamy brown in color and have an intense, sweet and spicy aroma. Its pungency is pronounced when the seeds are ground or crushed, and it tends to dominate the flavors in a dish. It is an essential ingredient in roasted or raw curry powder mixes. Freshly roasted ground cumin has an exotic and nutty aroma. Sprinkled on **Cucumbers in Yogurt** (p. 54), it provides an elegant finish to the dish. In **Eggplant Raita** (p. 70), ground cumin is lightly fried in oil and added as a final garnish, a unique way of bringing out the best in this tiny seed.

curry leaves (*Murraya koenigii*). Curry leaves are a big part of flavoring in Sri Lankan and South Indian cooking. This popular ingredient is now available in many parts of the world in fresh, dried, or freeze-dried form. Curry leaves have a slightly bitter, orange taste and a warm curry flavor that cannot be duplicated by any other ingredient. They are used raw in freshly ground relishes and sambals, chopped or minced in marinades, and cooked in curries. Past practice was to discard the curry leaves before serving, but this is no longer done and is also considered old-fashioned. One reason is that the medicinal value of the curry leaf has become widely known, and as it is not as coarse as bay leaf, many prefer to eat it. **Curry Leaf Sambal** (p. 174) and other preparations are popular accompaniments due in part to their medicinal value. Another reason is that chefs regard curry leaves floating in a curry as a natural garnish that is pleasing to the eye and awakens taste buds.

dal. The three broadly defined categories of legumes are lentils, beans, and peas. All are referred to as "dal."

deglaze. To swirl or stir a liquid, usually wine, stock, or fruit juice, in a pan to dissolve caramelized food particles remaining on the bottom. The resulting mixture becomes the base for a sauce.

demi-glace. Sauce made of equal parts stock and brown sauce cooked until reduced by half.

Dijon grainy mustard. See **prepared mustard**

dill (*Anethum graveolens*). The dill plant has delicate, bluish-green, feathery leaves with a sharp parsley and anise taste. Dill is best used fresh, as the aroma is lost during the cooking process. **Dill seeds** are flat, oval, and brown. They are almost always used whole. The seeds are slightly bitter and have a peppery aroma with a hint of fennel. Fresh dill and dill seeds are used in Scandinavian cooking. They are both good in pickles and relishes (see **Dill Raita,** p. 90).

dosa. The batter for these fluffy pancakes (also known as thosai) is made of soaked urad dal and rice and enriched with fried back mustard seeds and other spices and herbs. The batter is fermented, which gives these delicious pancakes a unique sour flavor.

dried ginger powder. See **ginger**

dried red chilies. See **chilies**

dried shrimp. These small, pinkish-orange dried shrimp, usually roasted and ground, are used as a flavoring in Asian dishes.

fennel seeds (*Foeniculum vulgare*). Fennel seeds are yellow-green and look like large cumin seeds that are flat, with ridges and fine hairy fibers. They are aromatic and have a sweet licorice taste. The seeds are used for their aroma and are available whole, ground, or roasted and ground. Roasted fennel seeds are more aromatic than raw seeds. They are used in curry powder blends, sausages, breads, cookies, and desserts.

fenugreek (*Trigonella foenum-graecum*). This exotic spice has a bitter taste and strong aroma. When cooked in oil or simmered in curries with coconut milk, it adds an unexplainable mystical aroma. It has a sophisticated bitter-sweet aftertaste, like burnt sugar. **Fenugreek seeds** are a standard spice in Indian and Sri Lankan curries and certain chutneys. Fresh or dried fenugreek leaves are widely used in Indian cooking.

fines herbes. A blend of herbs used for seasoning in French cuisine, it typically includes chervil, chives, parsley, and tarragon, as well as other herbs.

fish sauce. A strong-smelling, salty, amber-colored, clear liquid made from shrimp, anchovies, and other small fish fermented in brine. Nam pla is a milder version; the stronger version is nuoc mam. Both are available in Asian grocery stores and supermarkets.

flavorings. The terms "flavorings" and "seasonings" are used interchangeably. A flavoring adds a new taste to food, thus altering its natural flavors. Sugar and vinegar are basic flavorings; tamarind, coconut milk, condiments, herbs, and spices are all flavorings.

garam masala. See **masala**

garlic (*Allium sativum*). Garlic is a member of the lily family. Chefs refer to it as the "lily of the kitchen," and it is loved and used around the world. There are different types of garlic: the common white-skinned garlic, as well as garlic with pink or purple skin. The garlic bulb is composed of several sections called "cloves." Each garlic clove is covered with a papery membrane that must be removed before using. Garlic is highly aromatic and has a strong flavor. It is used raw, cooked, and baked in sauces, with broiled and grilled meat, with pasta, and in pesto, garlic butter, and salad dressings. It can be rubbed inside salad bowls and even roasted and tossed in honey. Along with ginger and onion, it is part of the indispensable flavor trinity of Asian and Indian cuisines.

Garlic is available dehydrated, in bits and slices, or powdered. **Garlic flakes,** another form of dehydrated garlic, are often used in South Asian food.

gherkins. Gherkins are small, dark green pickling cucumbers harvested before they ripen and pickled in vinegar. Cornichons, very tiny pickled cucumbers, are a traditional French accompaniment to pâté.

ginger (*Zingiber officinale*). Ginger (also known as gingerroot) has a tan skin and green-yellow, moist, fibrous flesh. It has a peppery hot taste with a hint of sweetness and a pungent, spicy aroma. Fresh ginger, peeled and sliced, flavors foods such as soups, seafood, and meats and is used, peeled and grated, in relishes and chutneys. It is a required flavor in many Asian and Indian dishes, especially beef and chicken curries. **Dried ginger powder** is made of fresh gingerroot dried and ground to a light buff-colored powder. It is piquant, slightly hotter than fresh ginger, and has an enticing, sweet fragrance. Ginger powder is used in dishes such as **Tamarind and Raisin Chutney** (p. 12) and in fruit compotes. It is also used extensively in baked goods.

Hawaiian chilies. See **chilies**

herbs. Herbs are a group of aromatic plants whose parts, such as leaves and flowers, are used as flavorings for food. Herbs may be used fresh or dried, cooked with certain foods, freshly chopped and sprinkled on cooked or uncooked food, or simply as a garnish. They introduce flavorings and aromatics to stocks, soups, stews, and sauces. Garlic, onion, and ginger, though not herbs in the true sense, are essential kitchen staples, known as the flavor trinity, that give immense flavor to food. Flavorings should not mask the taste or aroma of the primary ingredient and, most importantly, should be in harmony with it and not overwhelm its taste.

horseradish (*Amoracia rusticana*). The horseradish plant is a member of the mustard family. Its root is similar to a parsnip in appearance and pungent in taste. It has a powerful nose-tingling smell and a fiery taste that is very sharp and biting. The root is peeled, grated, and used in horseradish sauce, a perfect accompaniment to rich or fatty meats such as the traditional prime rib and fish such as mackerel, smoked trout, and tuna. Homemade horseradish sauce is more pungent than the store-bought variety. To make a quick horseradish sauce, whisk to soften ½ cup of sour cream, fold in 1 tablespoon (15 ml) of freshly grated horseradish, and season with vinegar, sugar, black pepper, and salt to taste.

jaggery. Jaggery, or palm sugar, is a coarse, honey-colored sugar derived by boiling down the sap of the palm (*Careota urens*) or coconut palm (*Cocos nucifera*). The resulting sugar is set into round molds. In taste, it is reminiscent of honey, chocolate, and caramelized sugar.

julienne. To cut food into strips about the size of matchsticks; also any food cut that way.

kabocha pumpkin (*Curcubita maxima*). The kabocha pumpkin (also known as kabocha squash) is a variety of pumpkin. It is small and has a dark green skin with light green and yellow streaks. The flesh is tender and orange with a sweet flavor.

ketchup. Ketchup (also called "catchup" and "catsup") is a popular condiment made with tomatoes, other fruits and vegetables, sugar, vinegar, and spices. It is glossy, with a thick consistency.

lemongrass (*Cymbopogon citratus*). Lemongrass has a strong yet pleasing lemony aroma. The bulb and tender inner part of the stalks are used to impart flavor to salads or cooked food. Lemongrass brightens and awakens flavors in preparations like sambal (see "**Seeni" Sambal,** p. 172).

lumpries. This elaborate Sri Lankan "meal in a packet" consists of fragrant savory rice, exquisite curries, and accompaniments tightly wrapped in a piece of fresh banana leaf and baked in the oven. The aroma trapped in the banana leaf is released when guests open their lumpries at the dinner table.

mace and nutmeg (*Myristica fragrans*). Mace and nutmeg are different parts of the seed of the nutmeg tree. Both spices have a pungent aroma. Mace is similar in flavor to nutmeg but is more refined; it is a little bitter, whereas nutmeg is sweeter.

Mace is made from the aril, the red membrane encasing the seed, which turns an orange-brown color when dried. It traditionally is used in charcuterie and gives a heavenly fragrance to creamy soups and seafood sauces, desserts such as cheesecake and lemon curd tart, and preserves. Mace is available whole, in blade form, or ground.

After the aril is removed, the nutmeg seed is dried until the shell is brittle. If the kernel inside rattles when the seed is shaken, it is a healthy one. Crack and discard the shell and use the kernel. Like mace, nutmeg partners well with creamy dishes and traditionally is added to béchamel, cheese and tomato sauces, dishes with spinach, risotto, and mashed potatoes. Nutmeg is also a traditional flavoring for baked goods such as cakes, cookies, and gingerbread and gives a distinctive taste to eggnog and creamy drinks.

makrut lime (*Citrus histrix*). These fragrant, dark green leaves are indispensable in Thai cooking. They have a piercing citrusy aroma. Use whole leaves in curries and sugar syrups and discard the leaves when cooking is done.

Maldive fish. This term refers to skipjack tuna fillets cured and processed in the Maldive Islands. The fish are dried to a hard wooden texture and require no refrigeration. This favorite flavoring item in Sri Lankan cooking is available coarsely ground or powdered in sealed packets. It gives a unique fishy flavor to food.

mango powder (*Mangifera indica*). Mango powder, or amchoor, is made from the tart, unripe fruit. The mangoes are peeled, sliced, sun-dried, and ground into a light brown powder. Slightly sweet and sour, its tangy taste is similar to tamarind or lemon juice. Mango powder is used to add that essential tang to marinades, soups, curries, relishes, and chutneys.

masala. The term "masala" refers to spice blends that are made with several spices, usually roasted or unroasted and ground to a fine or coarse texture. Some are blends of whole spices and are used in stocks and even curries when the spices will not present problems with chewing. The recipes for **garam masala** (p. 226) and **chaat masala** (p. 227) feature roasted and ground spices.

masoor dal. These pink or salmon-pink lentils are also known as red lentils. The small, lens-shaped lentils cook quickly and do not need to be soaked in advance.

milk rice. This dish is known in Sri Lanka as kiri bath, meaning "milk rice." The rice is cooked in coconut milk until it is soft, seasoned with salt, and spooned onto a platter. Then it is shaped into a round, flat cake and cut into large diamond shapes. Milk rice is served on New Year's Day to augur prosperity for the coming year. In many homes, it is also served at breakfast on the first day of each month, usually with a hot sambal.

mint (*Mentha piperita*). There are many varieties of mint in the Labiatae family. Spearmint is also known as garden mint and, true to its name, grows wild in many gardens. As an herb, it can stand alone and is confined to specific dishes such as fruit, fruit salads, chocolate, and lamb. Mint is a preferred and widely used herb in the cooking of India, Sri Lanka, and the Middle East. In these countries, it appears in accompaniments to rich rice dishes, dips, sambals, and relishes. In many homes, mint is grown in pots and is available year-round. It is easy to find fresh and is also sold in dried form.

mirin. This Japanese rice wine is sweet and syrupy. It is used in sauces and marinades.

mung beans. Mung beans (also known as moong dal) are available whole or split. Split mung beans are hulled and are shiny and creamy yellow in color.

mustard oil. Mustard oil is pressed from the seeds of the brown mustard plant. It is uniquely pungent and has good preserving qualities. This aromatic oil is used extensively in the northern regions of India and Sri Lanka. It lends its unique aroma to oil-based pickles.

mustard seeds (*Brassica* spp.). These are the tiny seeds of the annual herb of the cabbage family that has an erect stem and yellow flowers. There are three different types of mustard plants: white, brown, and black. The seeds have no smell until they are crushed, ground, or cooked, when they release their characteristic taste, pungent and hot with a tangy bitterness.

nonreactive. This term describes utensils and equipment made of materials that do not react with acids and brine to cause discoloration in foods or form toxic substances.

nutmeg. See **mace and nutmeg**

onion. Onions are among the intensely aromatic and strong-flavored bulbous vegetables of the lily family (*Allium*). They are loved and used in cuisines around the world. The taste ranges from sweet to mild and from strong to pungent. They all have a stiff papery outer skin that is peeled off and discarded. Skin colors range from white, to yellow, to bright golden yellow. Red onions have a purplish-red skin and white-and-purplish-pink flesh and are ideal for using raw. Onions are used in numerous ways: cooked in stocks and sauces, roasted, grilled, stuffed and baked, pickled, and sliced raw in salads and relishes. Onions are also available as **onion flakes,** a sliced dehydrated form that is often used in sambals.

pachadi. This South Indian vegetable or fruit preparation has a yogurt base and is fragrant with spices, mainly black mustard seeds fried in mustard oil. To fry mustard seeds, vegetable oil and olive oil are good substitutes.

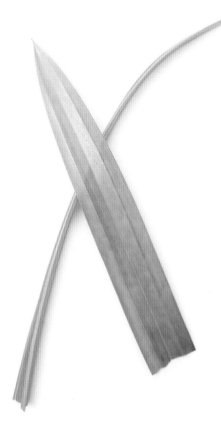

pandanus leaf (*Pandanus odoratissimus*). The pandanus plant has very long, saw-edged leaves with a fragrance reminiscent of pine. The leaves are used in Sri Lanka, Malaysia, and Indonesia as a flavoring for rice and curry dishes and are discarded after cooking. A 2-inch (5 cm) piece of fresh pandanus leaf will flavor 2 to 3 cups (500 to 750 ml) of rice.

panko. These Japanese bread crumbs are available with a fine or coarse texture. They are used as a coating for baked or deep-fried food.

paprika (*Capsicum annum*). Paprika is a smooth powder made by grinding dried sweet red peppers. Good-quality Hungarian and Spanish paprika have distinctive strong flavors, ranging from pungent to sweet. Hungary's national spice is an essential for the famous Hungarian goulash. Outside of Hungary and Spain, most versions of this spice are mild and without much taste. Paprika gives a red hue to food, ranging from light to dark depending on how much is used. It may be sprinkled on prepared food as a garnish.

pectin. A gelatinous carbohydrate obtained from certain fruits, it is used to thicken jams and jellies.

pennywort (*Centella asiatica*). Pennywort is also known as gotukola in Singhalese. In English, its common name is Asian pennywort. Gotukola is known to relieve arthritis pain and is sold in nurseries as an "arthritis herb." The green, quarter-size leaf with slightly crinkled edges is attached to a wiry hollow stem and has a mildly bitter, tangy taste. The leaf commonly is used in a sweetened beverage in Asian countries. It is at its best in a salad, such as **Pennywort "Gotukola" Sambal** (p. 167). In this recipe, pennywort leaves and stems are shredded fine, mixed with coconut, and seasoned with ground spices, lime juice, and salt, which transform the bitterness of the leaves into a sweet and tangy, deliciously enticing taste.

peppercorns. Peppercorns are the fruit of the pepper plant, plucked off the vine when they are ripe and red and yellow in color.
    Black peppercorns are dried until the husks are black and wrinkled. They are available whole; ground fine, medium, or coarse or cracked. The peppercorns may also be freshly ground onto salads and other cooked food. Freshly ground black pepper is refreshing

on ice cream, sliced strawberries, and fresh pineapple. Creamy goat cheese lightly crusted with cracked black pepper is divine in a spinach salad.

White peppercorns are ripe pepper berries that undergo a process of soaking, scarification, and husking. The creamy white peppercorns are ground and are available as white pepper. The flavor of white pepper is not as rich and aromatic as black pepper's, but it is almost as hot and commonly is used with creamy white sauces, butter sauces, and creamed potatoes.

Green peppercorns are the unripe berries of the pepper plant. They are available pickled or freeze-dried. They have a sour flavor, similar to the taste of capers, which makes them an excellent seasoning for fish and certain relishes.

pickles. Pickled cucumbers are the most common kind of pickle and are available whole, in wedges, sliced, or chopped. Varieties range from sweet to sour, spiced with chilies, peppercorns, cloves, and garlic or flavored with dill, tarragon, and bay.

pomegranate (*Punica granatum*). The pomegranate is a large fruit with a deep-pink to red-blush leathery skin and many juicy jewel-like seeds encased in translucent, deep-pink flesh. **Pomegranate seeds** are separated by bitter yellow membranes, but their flesh is sweet and tart. Fresh pomegranate seeds have become a favorite with chefs and are used in many ways. Fresh whole seeds are sprinkled on salads and relishes.

Sun-dried pomegranate seeds turn a deep, dark red-wine color and are sticky, due to the dried juice enclosing the seed. Sun-dried pomegranate seeds have always been a popular spice in India, especially in the north. Whole sun-dried pomegranate seeds are used in stuffings for Indian breads. In the Middle East, they are sprinkled on hummus, fruit salads, and sweets. Whole sun-dried seeds are ground with other spices for **Chaat Masala** (p. 227), which is sprinkled on salads and relishes, flavors batter-fried vegetarian bites, and serves as a souring agent in food in place of lime and lemon juice.

Bottled **pomegranate molasses** and **pomegranate juice** are also generally available.

poppadom. These dried lentil wafers, mildly or highly spiced, are available in packets in Asian grocery stores. They should be deep-fried or grilled over low heat before they are served.

prepared mustard. Prepared mustard, sometimes called "made mustard," is a condiment made from one or more kinds of powdered mustard seeds, water, vinegar or wine, and other seasonings. Dijon, France, is the mustard capital of the world. Of all the varieties of prepared mustard, **Dijon grainy mustard** is a favorite around the world. It is made from ground and slightly crushed black or brown mustard seeds and has a very distinctive earthy taste, hot and nutty.

quinoa. Quinoa is a bead-shaped, cream-colored grain with a bland flavor. It was a staple of the ancient Incas. This popular grain is high in protein and is prepared like rice, with dried fruit and nuts added to compensate for its lack of flavor. It is also used in stuffings or cooked with other grains.

rehydrate. The process of restoring moisture that was lost during the drying process.

relish. This table condiment is a heavy, pickled "sauce" made with vegetables or fruit. It can be slightly sweet or savory, smooth or coarse, and hot or mild.

rice wine vinegar. See **vinegar**

rosemary (*Rosmarinus officinalis*). Rosemary has needlelike leaves and woody stems. It has a highly aromatic camphor and pine aroma. Rosemary is a common herb and is best used fresh; the dried form tastes woody and musky. Rosemary adds flavor and aroma to roasted and grilled meats and roasted potatoes; partnered with garlic, it adds a special taste sensation to roast lamb.

roti. A general term for bread, which can take many forms, whether made from ground grain, wheat, rice, or corn. Roti can be thin or thick, plain or with grated coconut mixed into the dough. It is usually eaten with a sambal.

sachet. A sachet is a cheesecloth bag filled with a blend of aromatic ingredients used to flavor stocks, sauces, soups, or stews. A standard sachet consists of parsley stems, cracked black peppercorns, thyme, bay leaf, and cloves. It is removed and discarded as indicated in each recipe after flavors have been extracted. See also **bouquet garni.**

saffron (*Crocus sativus*). The most expensive spice in the world, saffron is the dried stamens of the saffron crocus. It is available in thread or powder form. In addition to its haunting fragrance, saffron adds a golden orange-yellow hue to food, and the threads speckle dishes such as elegant saffron rice. Saffron should be soaked in hot water or hot milk before use and should be used sparingly. If overdone, it tastes medicinal and gives the dish a garish look.

salt (sodium chloride). Salt is the most basic and indispensable of seasonings used in food preparation. It is also a table condiment. Salt is odorless but has a strong, distinctive taste. It enhances the flavors of food and also acts as a preservative. There are many forms of salt available, and they vary in flavor and degree of salt-iness. Iodized salt provides iodine, an important nutrient. Rock salt facilitates freezing, and kosher salt also preserves food. Sea salt, which is a favorite of chefs, is good for cooking and as a table salt. Salt is temperature sensitive: the cooler the food, the saltier it tastes. When salting hot food that is meant to be served chilled, it is necessary to underseason.

samosa. This deep-fried triangular Indian pastry is stuffed with a mixture of meat or vegetables and pungent herbs. It is served with a green or tamarind chutney.

seasonings. Seasonings enhance the natural flavors of food without changing much of its original taste. Among many items in this category are salt and pepper, two of the most common and indispensable seasonings.

sesame seeds (*Sesamum indicum*). The seeds from sesame pods are tiny, flat, and oval in shape. They have a nutty, slightly sweet, rich taste. Sesame seeds are creamy white, brown, or grayish yellow in color. Black sesame seeds are a special variety of sesame seed. Sesame seeds are an ingredient in many cuisines, roasted and used as a garnish, sprinkled on breads and crackers, and ground to a paste known as **tahini** that is used to make hummus.

shrimp paste. This pungent paste is made from dried shrimp and is used mainly in Asian cooking.

soy sauce. An all-purpose condiment made with cooked soybeans, roasted wheat or barley, and salt. Its color ranges from pale brown to dark brown. Light soy sauce is thinner, and dark soy sauce is thicker and rich in flavor. Soy sauce is generally salty, but low-sodium versions are available. Soy sauce is used extensively in Asian cuisines, especially Japanese and Chinese, as a flavoring condiment.

spices. Spices are derived from aromatic plants or plant parts such as roots, barks, fruits, buds, flowers, flower parts, seeds, stems, leaves, and gum resins. They are available dried, ground, or whole. A large variety of spices is used to preserve food. Spices create distinctive flavors, fragrances, and aromas that give special character to food. Most also have medicinal qualities.

star anise (*Illicium verum*). The dried star-shaped fruit of the Chinese magnolia. Star anise seeds have a pungent aroma and a bitter licorice flavor and are the leading spice in Chinese five-spice powder. It is available whole or ground.

sugar. Sugar is a flavoring that is also used for preserving food. Granulated sugar is refined sugar that comes in fine, uniform crystals and serves many purposes throughout the kitchen. Brown sugar, both dark and light, is also a refined sugar with molasses added for color. Castor sugar is superfine granulated sugar and dissolves easily. Powdered sugar, also known as confectioner's sugar, is often used in bakeries for icings and glazes.

tahini. See **sesame seeds**

tamarind (*Tamarindus indica*). Tamarind is a flavoring ingredient. The tropical tamarind tree bears fruit in cinnamon-brown pods with brittle shells and is native to India. When the fruit is ripe, the chocolate-brown pulp separates easily from its shell and has a sweet lemony-date flavor. It has been a standard flavoring ingredient in India, Sri Lanka, and Indonesia since ancient times and has become a favorite in Western kitchens, too. Tamarind is used as a souring agent in certain curries, sambals, chutneys, and relishes. Use **nonreactive** utensils and strainers when preparing tamarind.

    Tamarind pulp is compressed into blocks and is available with or without seeds. To use compressed tamarind, break off a portion of the block, about 2 tablespoons (30 ml), and place it in a bowl. Pour 1 cup (250 ml) of hot water into the bowl and set aside for 15 minutes. With your fingers, mash up the tamarind and extract as much pulp as possible. Strain tamarind pulp and transfer to a fresh container; discard fiber and seeds if any. Pour into a sterilized jar, cover, and store in the refrigerator. Thick tamarind pulp is deeply acidic and can be thinned with water to dilute to taste. Tamarind is available as a concentrate and should be mixed with hot water as required. **Tamarind juice** is also available bottled.

tarragon (*Artemisia dracunculus*). Tarragon is an essential herb in French cuisine. Its leaves are long and narrow and a dark green color. It has a sweet, strong aroma and goes well with tomatoes and goat cheese.

thyme (*Thymus vulgari*). Thyme is a popular herb with tiny gray-green leaves and small purple flowers on woody stems. The leaves have a strong, slightly lemon-balm-like aroma. The herb complements seafood and vegetables and adds flavor to stocks and sauces. When using thyme with seafood, pull leaves off the woody stems, chop the leaves, and use as needed. Whole thyme sprigs, fresh or dried, may be added to sauces and stocks that are meant to be strained.

turmeric (*Curcuma longa*). A substitute for saffron, turmeric is known as "poor man's saffron" and gives food a yellow color. It has a pleasing woody aroma and taste and should be used sparingly, to add a delicate blush to food; if overused, it can be garish and bitter.

umami. Refers to a savory, meaty flavor, one of the five basic taste sensations.

urad dal. Also known as the black gram bean, urad dal is available whole or split. Split urad dal can be purchased "washed," meaning the beans are hulled and cleaned and are ivory in color.

vinegar. Vinegar is a preservative and a cooking ingredient that flavors food. There are various kinds of vinegar. **Apple cider vinegar** is made from unpasteurized apple juice or cider and has a fruity aroma. It is less acidic compared to other vinegars and is the vinegar of choice for many fruit chutneys. Dark, syrupy, and sweet, **balsamic vinegar** is made from concentrated grape juice aged from four to fifty years in barrels of oak, cherry, mulberry, and juniper wood, which gives the vinegar its characteristic flavor, texture, and color. True balsamic vinegar is extremely expensive, but commercial products imported from Italy are affordable and available. White balsamic vinegar is good in relishes and salad dressings. **Coconut vinegar** is made from either coconut water or the sap of the coconut palm. This exotic vinegar is also excellent for making cooked chutneys. **Distilled vinegar** produced from grain alcohol is clear and has a strong flavor. Its high acid content makes it the preferred vinegar for pickling and preserving. Flavored vinegars are traditional vinegars infused with herbs, spices, berries, fruits, or vegetables. Malt vinegar made from barley is rich and mildly sweet and is a preferred condiment with fried snacks such as chips. **Rice wine vinegar** is sweet and clear and has a refined taste. In combination with sugar, it seasons rice for sushi and is ideal for relishes, dressings, and flavor-enhancing syrups. **Wine vinegars** are made from red and white wine, sherry, and champagne. These vinegars are preferred in Continental and Mediterranean cuisines.

white mustard seeds (*Brassica alba*). White mustard seeds are sand- or amber-colored and larger than black and brown mustard seeds. They are milder, with a sweet tang, and are a component of pickling spices. They are also available as a powder, blended with other additives, and are used in prepared mustard.

white pepper. See **black pepper**

wi apple (*Spondias cytherea* Sonn., also *Spondias dulcis* Parkinson). This fruit is also referred to as Tahitian quince and is indigenous to Polynesia. The fruit, popular in Asia, is plum-shaped, sweet and sour, and eaten at all stages of ripeness. Its distinguishing feature is a spiny seed. The spines toughen as the fruit matures.

winter melon (*Benincasa hispida*). Winter melon, a large gourd, is also known as ash pumpkin. It has an ash-like powdery coating on its skin and is available in markets cut into quarters or smaller pieces. It can be made into preserves, candied to produce crystallized sweets, and cooked in savory dishes, such as the famous Chinese winter melon soup.

Index

Africa, 125, 233
ajwain, 232
Apple and Lemon Marmalade, 196
Apricot Dip, 220
asafetida, xiv, 27, 225, 229

Baba Ghanoush, 47
Banana Relish, 27, 38, 223
bay leaf, 230, 231, 247
Bengali Spicy Tomato "Pachadi," 55
bird's eye chili, 2, 29, 233
bitter melon, 230; Bitter Melon Pickles, 125; Bitter Melon Sambal, 183; Fried Bitter Melon Sambal, 180
"Blachan," 156
Black Bean Salsa, 30
Black Bean, Mango, and Pineapple Salsa, 30
black mustard seeds, 225, 230, 231, 243
black pepper, xvii, 244–245, 247
Black Plum Chutney, 9
black rice, 42, 231
black sesame seeds, 75, 78, 248
Blood Orange and Mint Relish, 78
Brandade, 77
Brandied Cherries, xv, 220
brazier, xix
Brie, 216
buriyani, 16, 159, 172, 231

cardamom, 195, 223, 224
carrot, 1; Carrot Marmalade, 208; Carrot, Orange, and Mint Relish, 33; Carrot Sambal, 163; Sweet Carrot Pickles, 137
cayenne pepper, 232, 233

Chaat Masala, 227, 232, 246
chana dal, 94, 173, 232
Charred Butternut Squash and Tomato Relish, 89
Charred Tomato Relish, 57
cheesecloth, 99, 101, 119, 247
Chermoula, 85
chilies, 233, 237, 239, 245
chutney, ix, xiv, xv, xvii, xx–25, 42, 225, 231, 238, 239, 242, 247, 249, 250; Black Plum Chutney, 9; Citrus Chutney, 6; Cranberry and Orange Chutney, 14; Date Chutney, 11; Dried Cranberry Chutney, 15; Festive Fruit Chutney, 10; Green Mango Chutney, 3; Green Tomato Chutney, 22; Green Tomato and Apricot Chutney, 22; Gooseberry Chutney, 18; Hawaiian Mango Chutney, 2; Hawaiian Star Fruit Chutney, 5; Hot Lime Pickles Chutney, 16; Kabocha Chutney, 25; Papaya Chutney, 19; Peach Chutney, 9; Pear and Ginger Chutney, 19; Tamarind and Raisin Chutney, 12; Tomato and Lemon Chutney, 21; Wi Apple Chutney, 16
cilantro. *See* coriander
cinnamon, 97, 195, 223, 226, 229, 234
Cinnamon-y Apple Pickles, 143
Citrus Chutney, 6
cloves, xv, 97, 245, 247
coconut, xiv, xv, 27, 147; chips, 78, 234; Coconut "Mallun," 187; Coconut Relish, 51; flakes, 170, 234; grated fresh, 27, 147, 234; Mango and Coconut Relish, 52; milk, 46, 57, 234; relish, xiv, 27, 51, 52, 63; vinegar, 75, 108, 235, 250
coriander, xv, 234, 235, 236
Cranberry and Orange Chutney, 14
crudité platter, 109, 137

crushed red pepper, 233, 236

cucumber: Cucumber, Onion, and Tomato Relish, 55; Cucumber Pickles, 109; Cucumber Relish with Coconut Milk Dressing, 72; Cucumbers in Yogurt, 54

cumin, 223, 225, 226, 227, 230, 236

Curried Mangoes, 192

Curried Pineapple, 190

Curry Leaf Sambal, 174, 236

curry leaves, 27, 225, 236

dal, roasted, 232

Date Chutney, 11

demi-glace, 145, 237

Deviled Potatoes, 160

Dijon grainy mustard, 237, 246

Dill Raita, 90, 237

distilled vinegar, 250

dosa, 27, 85, 237

Dravidians, 41

Dried Cranberry Chutney, 15

dried ginger powder, 237, 239

dried red chili, 97, 233, 237

dried shrimp, 147, 237, 248

duck, 205; *à l'orange*, 6; confit, 200

Easy Flavor Sprinkler, 174

eggplant: Eggplant "Pahi," 132; Eggplant Raita, 70, 236; Eggplant Relish, 46

Fast Mustard Pickles, 113

Fast Pickled Fruit, 112

fennel and fennel seeds, 237

fenugreek, 97, 238

Festive Fruit Chutney, 10

fish sauce, 147, 237

France, 77

Fresh Apple Relish, 35

Fresh Coriander Relish, 85

Fried Bitter Melon Sambal, 180

Fried Eggplant and Cashew Sambal, 179

Fried Eggplant and Yogurt Relish, 45

Fruit "Chaat Masala," xv, 29

frying pan, xviii, xix, 224, 225

garlic, xvii, 1, 229, 238, 239, 247; flakes, 238; roasted, 64, 77, 238

ginger, xv, xviii, 1, 97, 147, 237, 239

gingerroot, 239

Gooseberry Chutney, 18

gotukola, 167, 244

Grated Carrot, Orange, and Raisin Relish, 48

Green Apple, Apricot, and Pecan Preserve, 207

Green Chili and Coconut Sambal, 159

Green Mango Chutney, xv, 3

Green Mango Pickles, 120

Green Tomato and Apricot Chutney, 22

Green Tomato Chutney, 22

Guacamole, 34

Handy Sweet Pickling Syrup, 136, 137

Harissa, 81

Hawaiian Fried "Haupia," 61

Hawaiian Chili Pepper Water, 29, 233

Hawaiian chilies, 2, 101, 233, 239

Hawaiian Lomilomi Salmon, 58

Hawaiian Mango Chutney, xv, 2, 3

Hawaiian Star Fruit Chutney, 5

heavy-bottomed pan, xviii, 16, 19, 67, 204, 205, 216

Herb Pesto, 62

Honey Roasted Baby Carrots, 189

hors d'oeuvres, 2, 9, 47, 102, 105, 106, 125, 136, 137

horseradish, 97, 235, 239

Hot Chili Sambal, 147, 159

Hot Green Cilantro Relish, xv, 27, 37

Hot Lime Pickles Chutney, 16

Hot and Spicy Lime Pickles, xv, 16, 101, 175

Hummus, 47, 246, 248

India/Indian: accompaniments, xiv; asafetida, 229; basmati, 230; black seeds, 230; breads, 232, 246; carom, 232; chilies, 233; chutney, 1; chutni, 27; dosa, 27; ginger, 239; mint, 242; mustard oil, 243;

pachadi, 243; pickles, 97; rice pilaf, 232; samosa, 247; tamarind, 12, 249
Indian Green Mango Pickles, 119

jaggery, 1, 147, 240
Jaggery Pickles with Fruit and Dates, 111
jelly, 195, 199, 244

Kabocha Chutney, 25
kabocha pumpkin, 25, 139, 240
Kapi'olani Community College, xi
King Kashyapa I, 192
Kumquat Preserve, 211
"Kuni" Sambal, 169

Leek and Tomato Sambal, 184
Lemon Curd, 216
Lime Pickle Sambal, 175
lomilomi salmon, 58
lumpries, 156, 241

mace, 195, 223, 241, 243
makrut lime, 216, 240
Maldive fish, 241
mango, xv, 1, 27; powder, 227, 242
Mango and Coconut Relish, 52
masala, xv, 225, 226, 227, 232, 238, 242, 246
masoor dal, 67, 242
Maui Onion Pickles, 122
meat, roasted, 119, 122, 124, 195; beef, 214; chicken, 102, 160, 196; lamb, xv, 193, 196, 213, 220, 247; pork, xv, 34, 106, 111, 144, 145, 196, 213; turkey, 9, 14
Mediterranean, 230, 236, 251
milk rice, 242
mint, 24
Mint and Coconut Relish, xiv, 63
Minty Cashew Pesto, 46, 63
mirin, 76, 242
Mountain Apple Relish, 37
Mung Bean and Coconut Relish, 51
mung beans, 243

nam pla, 237
nonreactive utensils, xvii, 1, 27, 97, 249
North Indian rice pilaf, 232
nuoc mam, 237
nutmeg, 97, 195, 224, 226, 229, 241
nuts, roasted, 35, 75, 89, 127, 170, 219;

Ogo Relish, 76
Okra Sambal, 151
onion, xvii, xviii, 1, 27, 147, 225, 233, 239, 243; flakes, 78, 170
Onion and Chili Pickles, 122
Orange and Date Relish, 46, 48
Orange, Fennel, and Red Onion Relish, 76

pachadi, 55, 243
Pakistan, xiv, 1
pandanus leaf, 244
Papaya and Pineapple Marmalade, 202
Papaya Chutney, 19
Papaya Salsa, 34
Parsley Sambal, 164
Peach Chutney, 9
Pear and Ginger Chutney, 19
Pear, Orange, and Date Preserve, 219
pecorino, 62
pennywort, 244
Pennywort "Gotukola" Sambal, 167, 244
pesto, 62, 230, 238; Herb Pesto, 62; Minty Cashew Pesto, 63; Pesto, 62
piccalilli, 27
pickles, 97–145
pickling, 27, 233, 235, 238, 243, 245, 246
Pickled Beets, 105
Pickled Cauliflower, 116
Pickled Cherries, 106
Pickled Grape Tomatoes, 105
Pickled Grapes, 106
Pickled Kumquats, 138
Pickled Okra, 125
Pickled Papayas, 128

Pickled Plums, 145
Pickled Pumpkin, 139
Pickled Radishes, 137
Pickled Red Onion Rings, 124
Pickled Stuffed Dates, 127
Pickled Watermelon Rind, 144
Pickled Whole Onions, 124
Pineapple and Lime Preserve, 216
Pineapple Pickles, 135
"Pol" Sambal, 152
pomegranate 245, 246; Pomegranate Relish, 41
Pomelo Relish, 75
poppadum, xiv, 42
Potatoes with Cucumber and Yogurt Dressing, 71
presentation, 33, 47, 170
Preserved Lemon Wheels, 199
Preserved Peaches, 201
Preserved Spicy Oranges, 205
preserves, 194–220
puree, 77

quinoa, 15, 246

Ranjit, G. C., v, xiii, 174
Red Onion Marmalade, 214
Red Pepper and Tomato Jelly, 199
Rhubarb and Green Apple Preserve, xv, 213
rice, roasted, 231
rice wine vinegar, 246, 251
Rice with Chickpeas, Raisins, and Cashew Nuts, 42
Ripe Mango Pickles, 119
Roasted Coconut Sambal, 152
Roasted Eggplant Sambal, 193
Roasted Garlic with Honey and Balsamic Vinegar, 64
rondeau, xix, 2, 6, 10
Rouille, 86

sachet, 6, 9, 144, 231, 249
Salted Lemon Wedges, 102
Salted Salmon, 58

sambal, ix, xiv, xv, 146–193, 233, 236, 241, 242, 243, 244, 247, 249; Banana Blossom Sambal, 176; Bitter Melon Sambal, 183; Carrot Sambal, 163; Curry Leaf Sambal, 174; Fried Bitter Melon Sambal, 180; Fried Eggplant and Cashew Sambal, 179; Green Chili and Coconut Sambal, 159; Hot Chili Sambal, 147, 159; "Kuni" Sambal 169; Leek and Tomato Sambal, 184; Lime Pickle Sambal, 175; Okra Sambal, 151; Parsley Sambal, 164; Pennywort "Gotukola" Sambal, 167, 244; "Pol" Sambal, 152; Roasted Coconut Sambal, 152; Roasted Eggplant Sambal, 193; "Seeni" Sambal, 172, 241; Spicy Fruit Sambal, 147, 148
samosa, 247
Sanskrit, 41
saucepot, xviii, 77, 211
sauteuse, xix
sautoir, xviii, xix, 3
seeds, roasted, 45, 48, 57, 71, 75, 82, 174, 230, 236, 237, 248
serrano chili, 108, 122
"Serundeng," 170
sesame oil, 97
sesame seeds, 248, 249
shallot, xvii, 27
shrimp, roasted, 35, 156, 237
Sicilian Hot Relish, 81
"Sinhala Achaharu," 108
South Asia, ix, 1, 27, 238
Southeast Asia, 231, 259
South Indian, 226, 236, 243
southern India, 232
Spiced Dal "On the Side," 67
Spiced Stuffed Pickled Lemons, 99
Spiced Yogurt, 94, 223
spices, 223–227
spicy, xv, 1, 27, 97, 147, 195, 233, 236, 239
Spicy "Chutney" Powder, 173
Spicy Fruit Sambal, 147, 148
Spicy Kumquat Preserve, 210

Spicy Pickled Lemon Slices, 100
Spicy Pickles, 109
Spicy Winter Melon Preserve, xv, 204
spinach, 27, 241, 245
Spinach Raita, 93
Spinach and Sour Cream Relish, 33
Sri Lanka, ix, xi, xii, xiii, xiv
stainless steel, xviii, xix, 77, 246
standby, 100, 179
star fruit, xx, 5
Stewed Rhubarb, 213
Stuffed Pickled Wax Peppers, 115
sun-dried, 97, 227, 242, 246
sweet, 1, 27, 97, 147, 195
Sweet Carrot Pickles, 137
Sweet Citrus Pickles, 113
Sweet Mango Relish, 35, 127
Sweet and Sour Beet Relish, 33
Sweet and Sour Pickled Pears, 140

tamarind, 1, 27, 147, 238, 242, 247, 249
Tamarind and Raisin Chutney, 12, 239

Tapenade, 82
thosai, 237
Three Relishes for Chips, 33
Tomato Confit, 200
Tomato Lemon Chutney, 21
Tomato Relish for Fried Okra, 68
Tomato Relish with Goat Cheese, 82
turmeric, xv, 250

umami, 27, 147, 250
underripe produce, xviii
urad dal, 51, 85, 173, 237, 250

vegetables, roasted, 90, 94, 189, 193, 211, 213,
    220, 225, 243

White Asparagus Vinaigrette, 131
wi apple, 251; Wi Apple Chutney, 16; Wi Apple
    Pickles, 143; Wi Apple Preserve, 219
winter melon, xv, 251

Zucchini "Mallun," 155

Kusuma Cooray, CCE, CHE, FCFA (CG), trained at Le Cordon Bleu; the National Bakery School, London; and École de Cuisine La Varenne, Paris. She obtained her technical training at Marks and Spencer Directors Dining Room, London, and Henri IV Restaurant, Chartres. She was awarded a scholarship by the School of Hotel Administration at Cornell University, where, as a guest lecturer, she shared her expertise in the cultures and cuisines of Southeast Asia.

Mrs. Cooray served as corporate chef for tobacco heiress Doris Duke and, later, executive chef for the renowned Honolulu restaurant The Willows. She has won several awards, including the Burton trophy for outstanding student, National Bakery School, London; the Brillat Savarin Medal of Honor, Confrérie de la Chaîne des Rôtisseurs; and, recently, the Gold Star of Excellence, Confrérie de la Chaîne des Rôtisseurs, in recognition of her contributions toward the education of young chefs in Hawai'i and the Pacific.

She is the author of *Burst of Flavor,* which highlights spices and harmonizing East-West flavors, and *From Ocean to Plate: Cooking Fish with Hawai'i's Kusuma Cooray,* both published by the University of Hawai'i Press. Both books won Ka Palapala Po'okela Awards for Excellence in Cookbooks.

Mrs. Cooray taught for twenty-eight years at the Culinary Institute of the Pacific, University of Hawai'i, and retired as Professor Emerita in 2015. She served as honorary consul for the Democratic Socialist Republic of Sri Lanka in Hawai'i for seventeen years and retired in 2017 as Dean Emerita.

The Chairman of the Joint Chiefs of Staff in Washington, DC, awarded her the Distinguished Public Service Award, which was presented to her by Admiral Harry B. Harris Jr., US Navy Commander, US Pacific Command, in March 2017.